BE FREE

LIVING THE
LIFE GOD HAS
ALWAYS
INTENDED FOR
YOU

Sam Lee

Be Free

Living the Life God has Always Wanted for You
by Sam Lee

Printed in U.S.A

ISBN: 978-0-9988854-9-0

Cover Design and Layout by Sakura Reese, Ahava Design

DEDICATION

This book is dedicated to Caryn Fugami. Caryn, who has gone on to be with the Lord, was my greatest cheerleader and encourager to pursue writing this book. I know she is smiling down on us as she witnesses this book finally come to pass.

ACKNOWLEDGEMENTS

I want to acknowledge God and the people He used to walk together with me to make this happen.

Denise Richardson – God brought me almost seven thousand miles to partner together with you. You were the missing piece to take this book the final nine yards. So grateful for your *amazing* work reorganizing, reworking and crafting what God initially had given me.

Hogan Lee – From encouraging me to never give up, to instilling faith in me, to reading and rereading, you were a friend that was closer than a brother throughout this process. Thank you for walking with me.

Barry Deguchi – My spiritual father who modeled and taught me so much of what is written in these pages. Words cannot express how grateful I am for you.

Marcy Binuya, Jon Hino, Todd Rettberg, and Damon Gohata – My first round and final round of beta readers. Thank you for your time and effort in reading and providing me with invaluable input.

My Catalyst Church Family – You were my partners, covering and source of strength in living out the freedom we have in Christ. You truly are my family.

Susan Lee – My wife and my hero. You've shown me what it means to persevere and trust in God. You are the reason I began this journey toward freedom. Grateful to God that I can walk with you now as a new man, husband and father.

TABLE OF CONTENTS

PREFACE

A CRISIS OF FAITH

After graduating from seminary and studying three and a half years of Greek, Hebrew and theology, I entered full-time ministry. I served at a church in Cerritos, California, as its small groups' pastor. My role was overseeing the small group ministry in the church.

It was a few years into my tenure as small groups' pastor that I was invited to attend a conference on evangelism. I thought this would be a great conference to attend. I could take what I learned and try to implement some of the ideas into the small groups at our church. But the conference took me in an entirely different direction.

I was at this conference enjoying the sessions when something happened to shake my foundation as a pastor and as a Christian. One of the main speakers was delivering a message on evangelism. One thing he shared that day has stayed with me for over twenty-five years.

He was talking about how Christians lived a privileged life. We were blessed by God. As a result, when we talk to a non-Christian, we should explain to them that the Christian life is like getting an upgrade. It's like when you are flying coach, but you get bumped up to first class. Or it's like when you are at a hotel, and they move you up to the penthouse. You get a major upgrade!

I understood the analogy, but I was troubled. I was troubled because what he said produced something unexpected within me. It produced doubt and insecurity. I started to wonder, "Is the Christian life really a major upgrade?"

I knew that the final destination for a Christian was a major upgrade. I knew that a life spent with God for all eternity was far better than an eternity spent apart from Him. I had no doubts about that. But what about before we die?

What about life on earth? Was a Christian's life on earth a major upgrade over a non-Christian's? That answer wasn't so clear to me. Remember I was a pastor at the time. I had gone to seminary. Yet if I was honest with myself, I couldn't answer "yes" with much conviction.

I looked at the lives of my non-Christian friends and wondered if my life was THAT much better than theirs. I looked at my non-Christian family and questioned whether the life I was living was that much of an upgrade over their lives. It wasn't as clear-cut as I would have liked, and it shook the foundation of my belief.

I left the conference with that nagging question stuck in my mind. I attended the conference with several other people from our church. When we got together to debrief, I didn't share about this moment. I never expressed my doubt to anyone.

When I look back at that time, I have one regret. I regret not voicing my doubts and asking God where this disconnect was coming from. God is not threatened by our questions. He isn't so insecure that He never wants us to express any doubts.

However, I wasn't able to push past my insecurity to ask why my life didn't match what the Bible claims the Christian life should look like. I didn't examine why I wasn't experiencing a major upgrade in my life.

I believe that my life suffered as a result of the decision to not question what was stirring in my heart and mind. I wish I would have had the courage to address the underlying issues that created these doubts. One area, in particular, that suffered as a result of brushing things under the rug was my marriage.

THREE-RING CIRCUS

Have you ever heard that when you get married that there are three rings? There is the engagement ring, the wedding ring, and then the boxing ring! For those that are married, you probably have evidence or scars that back this up. Sometimes married life can be a three-ring circus!

I'm the firstborn in my family. If you know anything about birth order, then you know one thing is true about firstborns. They are always used to having their own way! They feel the need to be right all the time. This stubborn determination can be a source of strength for firstborns. It also can cause problems.

Those problems can multiply when you put two firstborns together who are both thinking they are right, at the same time. Yes, you guessed correctly, my wife is also a firstborn. And when we got married, we often bumped heads.

We would have disagreements and neither of us was willing to back down. Both of us firmly believed that we were right and of course that the other person was wrong.

What happens when you have two immovable objects crashing together? Sparks fly! As the two of us held onto being right, our small arguments would snowball into bigger ones.

After having this happen repeatedly, we started noticing a pattern developing. We knew this pattern would happen, but we couldn't stop it. We felt powerless to break the cycle.

Often it would start very innocently. My wife would mention something and would try to communicate it as nicely as possible. She would say something like, "I notice you are really busy, but can you take out the trash? It's really starting to smell in here."

Again, she would say this very calmly and sensitively, but I would still get really upset. I would get very defensive. I would reply (not as calmly), "Well how come you didn't do these other things around the house?"

After I poked her with this verbal stick, she would respond, "How come you didn't do this other thing I asked you to do? I'm busy taking care of all these other things." And I would come back with, "Oh yeah, I did this, this and this." We would start comparing our laundry lists of all the things that we do in order to prove that we were working harder than the other person.

It doesn't take long to realize that this never works. No one wins this argument. Feelings get hurt and words are spoken that you later regret. We apologize and forgive. But when you are caught in this cycle, you feel discouraged and hopeless.

BREAKING THE CYCLE

I'm a thinker by nature, so I tried to analyze our arguments. I started to see that the majority of our arguments started out with something small, but ended up being knock-down, drag-out arguments. It started to become evident that there was something else happening.

I realized that the surface issue (like taking out the trash) was not the real problem. Something else was happening that made these arguments escalate. When it got more heated, it no longer was about taking out the trash. We were now arguing about something different—something more serious, something below the surface.

As much as we tried to break the cycle of what was happening in our marriage, we were at a loss. We read books, talked to friends, got counsel and prayed for wisdom. Yet, we were spiraling. Our arguments got more frequent and more heated.

The frustrating part was that we could see them coming. We could see the pattern repeating itself, but we couldn't stop it. It was like watching the same movie play over and over. We could not rewrite the script. It kept playing out just like before.

The results were damaging. With each argument, we distanced ourselves more and more. It was self-preservation. We had to guard our hearts because it wasn't safe. We didn't trust each other with our hearts any longer and as a result we grew distant.

Because of my anger and defensiveness, my wife had to walk around on egg-shells. She became hesitant to share her true feelings in fear of how I would react. When she did share, it was because things had come to a boiling point for her. You can imagine how that turned out.

Worse yet, it was impacting our children. As much as we tried to hide it, they could see and HEAR that things were not right between us. It created an environment that left them feeling insecure. Something desperately needed to change.

Then something did change. God stepped in. He showed me what I was pray-ing and pleading for Him to reveal. However, it wasn't what I was expecting to hear. It surprised me. I never would have guessed that what He had shown me would be the turning point in our marriage.

He showed me that something was indeed happening below the surface. It was the reason my life and my marriage were not flourishing. I came to recognize the source of my insecurity and anger.

I eventually realized this same underlying issue was behind all my doubts that I had many years earlier at that conference. What I learned dramatically changed my life, and I hope it will change your life too.

What I want to share with you in this book is a journey to freedom. It's a journey to experience the life that God has always intended for you and I to have. It's a life of freedom and joy.

My prayer is that as you read this book, you will be unchained to experience the newness of life God created us for. It's a life that we've hungered for and desired our entire lives, and it's available right now. All it takes is the willingness and courage to look beneath the surface to see what is preventing you from being free.

Author's Note: I share many stories throughout this book with the permission of each individual; however, I have changed the names and some details to protect their privacy. I've also added other stories to illustrate how this process works and how you can apply the principles in this book.

I quote many verses from the Bible (from the NIV, unless otherwise noted). I would encourage you to look up those verses on your own. Throughout the book, I will ask questions to apply to your life. Even though there is space to write things down, it would be good to have a notebook or journal handy to write down your thoughts and feelings as you read.

FAULTY **FOUNDATION**

WHAT'S UNDER YOUR HOUSE?

Imagine a beautiful, new house with a large backyard. You've just bought this house and it was designed just for you. However, in the backyard someone has buried two gigantic, radioactive boulders.

These boulders have been buried underground for a long time. How long? No one really knows, but it seems like the boulders have always been there. The boulders are not visible. When you look at the backyard, you can't even tell that the boulders are there.

Once you move into the house you start noticing that something is wrong. After years of living in this house, you start feeling sick. The longer you live in this house, the worse you feel. You start thinking that there's something wrong with you. Then, you see that your neighbors are getting sick too. You have a feeling that there is something wrong with your house, so you have it tested.

Men in HAZMAT suits come out and they run some tests. To your surprise, they discover trace evidence of radioactive material in your house. They continue to search and try to find the source of the contamination.

They go outside to your backyard. Their instruments detect something big. They tell you that they've never seen a reading this high. They tell you that there are two huge, radioactive boulders buried deep underground. They are the source of all the radioactivity in your house. The boulders are the reason why everyone is ailing.

At first, you're relieved. You thought that there was something seriously wrong with you. You had spent a tremendous amount of time, energy and money going to doctors and specialists trying to figure out the problem. They had no answers. The best they could do was to give you some pills to help manage your symptoms.

Soon after, your relief turns into panic. How can you go on living in this contaminated house? How are you going to recover from all this exposure to radioactive material? Are you doomed to live the rest of your life in this sickened state? Will your condition continue to get worse?

It's at this point the men in the HAZMAT suits tell you there's good news. They have developed a new technology that deals with the radioactive material. With this new technology, it's actually very easy to remove the radioactive material. It's so simple that you can do it yourself! You are grateful because it sounded like an expensive procedure to have these boulders removed!

They tell you that you don't have to go to doctors anymore and you can stop taking all those pills. Once the boulders are removed, the effects of the boulders will slowly diminish. They assure you that you will be completely fine and you can live a free and joyful life from now on.

The house is an analogy for our lives. The radioactive boulders, that are causing us to get sick, are things below the surface, in our thinking. It's a pattern of thinking we've developed and lived with our entire lives that is wreaking havoc. What is this pattern of thinking?

Throughout life, we are taught that our value comes from what we do and how others see us. These boulders represent how we see ourselves and how we develop our sense of identity.

These are deeply rooted beliefs that we may not even be aware of. However, if these ideas persist, they will continue to skew our sense of identity. Let's take a closer look at this pattern of thinking that we've developed. We'll start by looking at what the Bible has to say about these boulders.

CHAPTER 1

WHAT BOULDERS?

In order to examine these boulders, or pattern of thinking, let's look at Philippians 3:4-8. The writer, Paul, encourages a church in Philippi by describing his experience with the "flesh."

> [4] though I myself have reasons for such confidence. If someone else thinks they have reasons to put confidence in the flesh, I have more: [5] circumcised on the eighth day, of the people of Israel, of the tribe of Benjamin, a Hebrew of Hebrews; in regard to the law, a Pharisee; [6] as for zeal, persecuting the church; as for righteousness based on the law, faultless. [7] But whatever were gains to me I now consider loss for the sake of Christ. [8] What is more, I consider everything a loss because of the surpassing worth of knowing Christ Jesus my Lord, for whose sake I have lost all things. I consider them garbage, that I may gain Christ.

What is Paul trying to communicate in this passage about the flesh? First of all, the flesh is not our skin or our body. *The flesh is a pattern of thinking developed from living life on our own, independent from God.*

When Paul talks about the flesh in v. 4, he says that we should not put confidence in it. He says this knowing full well it would be easy for him to do so, even more than his readers.

Why does he say it would be easy for him to trust in his flesh or ability? It's because of his pedigree, education, and accomplishments listed in v. 5 and 6. He was the top of the top, Hebrew of Hebrews and an elite member of an elite group—the Pharisees.

Yet Paul says he puts no confidence in the flesh despite being a very well-educated, disciplined person, who followed after God with a zeal and passion that would have been praised by his fellow Jews. He had every reason to trust in his own ability, background and training to live out the Christian life.

But he considered all these successes garbage (literally dung) so that he may gain Christ (v.7, 8). In other words, he could not gain Christ if he continued to rely on his performance and success, even though he was extremely good at it!

Remember, Paul is speaking to people who are *already* Christians when admonishing them to not trust in their flesh. It's clear this apostle thinks the flesh represents a huge stumbling block in our lives even *after* becoming a Christian. We see that the flesh represents trusting in our own ability and performance apart from God. It is this *performance-based thinking* that the Bible is warning us against.

BUILDING A RELIGIOUS BOULDER

Let's take a short but revealing litmus test. It starts with a relatively simple question, "Does reading the Bible and praying draw us closer to God?" Simple, right? What would you say?

You might say, "Yes, of course it does! Reading the Bible and praying are essential in drawing us closer to God and His presence." Unfortunately, that's wrong. *Reading the Bible and praying do not draw us closer to God.*

STOP THE PRESSES! What?!? Before you go back and reread that last sentence, you did read it correctly. It's not a typo. I wrote it because I believe it's true. Now before you throw this book into the trash (or into the fire!), let me explain.

I'm **not** saying we shouldn't be reading the Bible and praying. I'm *not* saying these aren't very vital to every Christian's life. <u>I LOVE</u> reading the Bible and praying. These are a huge part of my life as a pastor and as a Christian. But we need to examine carefully what these things do for us.

What exactly does Bible reading and prayer accomplish? They help us to *enjoy the presence of God we **already** have because of Jesus.* We cannot be any closer to God than what Jesus provided for us. Because of Him, God's Spirit is literally living inside of us (see 1 Corinthians 3:16)!

Bible reading and praying do not serve to draw us closer to God and His presence in our lives. Reading the Bible and praying are great things, but we must be clear about this fact.

These activities, no matter how essential they are, do not replace what Jesus did for us in dying for our sins. The only reason we have the ability to come into God's presence and be close to Him is because of Jesus' work on the cross. It's not based on our performance.

PHARISEES, PHARISEES

If reading the Bible and praying did draw us closer into God's presence, then people in the Bible like the Pharisees would be very close to God. There was no one more adept at reading the Bible, praying and performing religious activities than the Pharisees. They were the standard bearers for what it meant to be faithful in reading the scripture and praying.

In fact, Jesus acknowledges this in Matthew 5:20. Here Jesus tells the crowd that their righteousness must exceed that of Pharisees in order to enter into the kingdom of heaven. The crowd would have known what that meant—"Impossible! There's no way. Not even on my best day. My righteous acts could not hold a candle to that of the Pharisees." And they would be right.

Isn't that the point? Isn't that what Jesus is driving at? He explains that no matter how much you read the scriptures or pray, you cannot enter into the kingdom of heaven. That is not the route that God chose to redeem His children and bring them into His presence.

Look at what Jesus says about the Pharisees, who were highly skilled in reading the Bible and praying, in Matthew 23:25, 27-28:

> [25] "Woe to you, teachers of the law and Pharisees, you hypocrites! You clean the outside of the cup and dish, but inside they are full of greed and self-indulgence. [27] "Woe to you, teachers of the law and Pharisees, you hypocrites! You are like whitewashed tombs, which look beautiful on the outside but on the inside are full of the bones of the dead and everything unclean. [28] In the same way, on the outside you appear to people as righteous but on the inside you are full of hypocrisy and wickedness.

Look at Jesus' assessment of the Pharisees. Does that sound like people that are really close to the heart of God and are in His very presence?

The Pharisees were doing all the right things on the outside, but on the inside they were "full of the bones of the dead and everything unclean." If reading the Bible and praying were God's prescription for how we can become close to Him, then the Pharisees would have been very intimate with God. However, this was Jesus' harsh assessment of them.

GOD PROVIDES IT ALL

If God provides everything for us to be intimate with Him, then why do we sometimes feel far from God when we don't read the Bible and pray? If we believe that Jesus is the only reason that we are able to be in God's presence, why do we rely on these spiritual activities to accomplish that?

The short answer: it's our flesh. It's our performance-based boulders. We've been conditioned to believe that we achieve success in our lives through our own hard work and effort. We then apply this same thinking to our Christian lives. *If we do the right things, God will be with us and pleased with us. Conversely, if we don't do the right things, then God will not be with us and not be pleased with us.*

We know that reading the Bible and praying don't make us Christians (there are non-Christians that read the Bible and pray). Yet, *after* we've become Christians, we do believe that these activities bring us into God's presence.

We want to believe that we are contributing something to this relationship we have with our Heavenly Father. How could He be close to us if we are not doing the right things? We believe we need to bring something to the table. We have trouble believing that even if we are not contributing anything, God is with us and loves us.

In reality, we bring nothing to the table. God brings it all. We have nothing. We offer nothing. We give nothing. What could we bring God to merit His presence and pleasure in our lives? The Bible says that our righteousness is like filthy rags (see Isaiah 64:6).

Through His son Jesus, God gave us His all. He gave everything necessary for us to not only be in relationship with Him but also to live out the Christian life (see 2 Peter 1:3). When we go back to our old pattern of thinking, we start reverting to the flesh. We start depending on ourselves and our performance. Subsequently, we create this religious, performance boulder.

DON'T GET ME WRONG

Of course, our actions are important. The Bible addresses the importance of the actions and choices we make (we will discuss this later in the book). Bible reading and prayer are an essential part of the Christian life. *If we don't read the Bible or pray, we would never get to experience the presence of God that Jesus died to give us.* That would be tragic.

Reading the Bible and prayer simply give us an opportunity to enjoy God's presence that we already have because of Jesus. You might say that's just semantics. However, the distinction is very important. We need to see that *our actions are a response to what God has done and not a replacement for what He's done.*

Reading the Bible and prayer are two of the avenues God chose to help us recognize, embrace, enjoy, relish and soak in God's presence in our lives. However, when we incorrectly believe that it's our actions that enable us to be present with God, then we'll always feel this heavy weight and responsibility on our shoulders.

This heavy weight actually prevents us from enjoying the presence we already have. We'll always have a nagging sense that we feel distant and that our intimacy with God is lacking. Instead of feeling secure about God's presence in our lives, we will constantly be wondering whether we have done enough.

THE 200 POUND COVER AND THE SPORTS PAGE

As long as we hold to this thinking, it will leave us feeling guilty and heavy-laden. Quiet time or devotions (the time we spend reading the Bible and praying), can feel like we are carrying a heavy weight on our shoulders. It is done in hopes that it will make us better Christians. We need to see how these performance boulders start negatively impacting things that are supposed to be enjoyable. Let's look at an example:

For some, when we look at our Bible sitting there on the table, we know we should open it up and read it. At the same time, we have the thought, "It's so hard for me to do it right now. Maybe I'll do it later." I've had this inner dialogue too many times to count.

But is opening the Bible really hard? Is putting your hand on the cover and pulling it open difficult? Does the cover weigh 200 pounds? Is reading the words on the pages difficult? Unless we have a disability holding us back, the answer is no. Then why at times does it feel so daunting?

I'm not a reader by nature, but I read all the time. You know what I read? The sports page. I read the sports page every day. Is opening up the sports page everyday a burden for me? Is it hard for me to do? Not at all. I enjoy it.

When I look at the sports page on the table, do I say to myself, "I *should* read it"? And if I haven't read it for a few days, am I overcome with guilt because I haven't done it? Do I tell myself, "I can't do it; maybe I'll do it later. Maybe I'll read the sports page tomorrow."

It sounds ridiculous but that's exactly how we approach reading the Bible. We want to read it, but at times we find it challenging to do. We feel the guilt of not having read it consistently. We feel overwhelmed by the pressure to keep it up. We feel the effects of the performance boulders we are carrying. That's what makes picking up the Bible, opening and reading it difficult at times.

When I read the sports page, I don't have any of these feelings. That's why it's so easy for me to pick it up and read it, even if I haven't read it in a long time.

That is not the case with the Bible. If I haven't read the Bible in a week or two, I carry guilt and responsibility on my shoulders to pick it up and read. It's the guilt and heaviness associated with reading the Bible that makes it so difficult to do on a regular basis.

We have to see that we don't bear the responsibility of maintaining our relationship with God. Jesus does this. We need to lift this heavy weight off our shoulders and give it back to Jesus. We can't carry this. *That's why sometimes Bible reading becomes a chore and not a pleasure.*

Instead of enjoying God's presence that we have because of Jesus, we try to earn and maintain it through our performance. Can you see the futility of trying to earn something that's already been given to us? No wonder, there are times reading the Bible seems more like regime or discipline than times of refreshing.

Even in doing good things, like reading the Bible, we can start developing this performance-based thinking. It can skew our experience of things that God established for our enjoyment.

WHERE DID THESE BOULDERS COME FROM?

Where does this type of thinking come from? How do these performance boulders first show up in our lives? Well, it starts from birth.

Even from the moment we enter this world, this performance thinking gets thrust upon us. Ever heard of an Apgar score? It's the score you receive when the doctors and nurses give you a test immediately after you are born (usually after one minute). They test for things like skin color, heart rate and reflexes. It's scored based on a scale that ranges from zero to ten. A score of ten means you are very healthy. A low score means you are not as healthy and are in need of immediate attention and help. From the very beginning we are evaluated and labeled!

As soon as my children found out there was an Apgar Score, they immediately wanted to know what their score was and how it compared with each other. They wanted to know if one scored higher than the other. Both my kids scored a ten out of ten by the way! Ha-ha, see how this thinking creeps its way in?

NO FREE LUNCHES!

I was eight years old. Our family was gathering to celebrate my paternal grandmother's birthday. My aunties, uncles, cousins, and grandmother met together at a Chinese restaurant. We were having a great time eating, talking, and laughing.

Then, suddenly a scene broke out. Maybe you've witnessed a scene like this. Maybe you've been a participant in a scene like this. We were dining in a side room of this restaurant when yelling started coming from our room. People were looking in and trying to see what was happening.

It was my Aunt Vicky and my dad arguing. What were they arguing about? It was a fight over who would pay for the bill. It was a back-and-forth battle. "I'm going to pay! No, I'm going to pay this time!"

It was a scene I had witnessed before, but it didn't make it any less embarrassing. Then as quickly as it started, it was over. My Aunt Vicky had emerged victorious. She tore the bill out of my dad's hand and ran out of the room to pay it!

Just when I thought the drama was finished, my dad called me over. He whispered in my ear, "Go under the table and put this money in your aunt's purse." I guess she left with only her credit card because her purse was hanging on her chair.

My dad put this wad of cash in my hand and sent me on my assignment. I really didn't know what was going on. I was just excited that I got to crawl on the floor without anyone yelling at me! Once at my aunt's chair, I put the money into her purse without anyone the wiser.

In the story above, my aunt was trying to bless our family by paying for the meal. My dad was not OK with this and had to remedy the situation. In his eyes, it wasn't right. He was the son and should be doing the paying. He didn't feel comfortable receiving without contributing.

The tragic part of this story was that my Aunt Vicky wanted to express her love to my dad, but he couldn't receive it. Not only did my dad not receive any blessing, but my aunt got robbed of the blessing of paying for the lunch. How could she have felt blessed after battling and arguing with my dad and then finding all that cash in her purse!

What is wrong with this picture? My aunt's heart was to love and bless my dad and her family. But because of this performance-based comparison, neither my dad nor my aunt left feeling good. Is this really the way God wanted this to unfold where no one leaves feeling loved or blessed?

Little did I know how much this incident, and others like it, impacted me and my thinking. When I became an adult, I found myself in similar situations. Especially as a pastor, people want to pay for my meal all the time. They do this because they want to bless me and show me how much they care about me.

But when the bill comes and they want to pay, I would protest. My performance-based thinking would not allow me to have them pay without doing something for them. I would find myself battling them for the bill. And even if they did end up paying the bill, I would need to say something like, "I'll get you next time." I needed to balance the scales.

Why did I feel the need to do this? When I fought people for the bill or told them that I'd pay the next time, didn't this affect my ability to receive their generous gesture? You bet it did. I didn't leave feeling blessed, taken care of or loved. I often felt guilty.

Guilty. Do you think that's what our friends or family desire when they treat us? And do you think they feel the blessing of treating us when we are protesting and we tell them we are going to pay them back? Does this diminish the joy of their giving? I think it does.

NOT SO MERRY CHRISTMAS

Frank and I have known each other since elementary school. We grew up together and were very close, but as we entered college, we lost touch. After many years, we reconnected again. Our families now get together around the holidays. In the past we've exchanged gifts for our kids around Christmas time.

One year we couldn't get together for Christmas, but we were able to meet several weeks afterwards in the new year. Our families got together for dinner and talked about everything that'd been happening in our lives. After dinner was finished, we were winding down our conversation and walked out to the parking lot. Then, something horrible happened.

Frank went to his car and pulled out a bag full of Christmas gifts for our kids. I was horrified! Since it was several weeks after Christmas, I didn't think we were going to exchange gifts for our kids. If you've ever been in this uncomfortable situation, you know what is coming next.

I was searching for what to say. Should I say that we left their kids' presents at home? No, that would be a flat-out lie. Should I apologize profusely? Should I lay myself on the mercy of the court? What do I do to save face?

I actually don't remember what I said, but I mumbled something. Frank is very observant, so he could tell I felt bad and told me that it was fine that we didn't have any gifts for his kids. You want to know what I was thinking after we left?

I was thinking, "How insensitive to give our kids gifts without telling us!" Seriously, this is what I was thinking! Just like the "No Free Lunches" story, this was not how things should have unfolded. I should have been extraordinarily blessed by their thoughtfulness. But was I overflowing with gratitude and thanksgiving? No, I was actually upset.

On top of that, Frank was definitely not feeling blessed after hearing my sad excuses and me constantly apologizing. I sucked all the joy of giving out of the situation. My performance-based boulder sucked the life from this time.

I couldn't just simply receive. I couldn't receive without having given anything in return. That just didn't sit right with me. Even though my friend was completely and genuinely fine, I couldn't be fine. Even though his family did this to make me and my kids feel loved, I didn't feel loved at all.

Funny thing is that my kids were overjoyed. They were very grateful and thankful. They hugged my friend and his wife. It wasn't a problem that we didn't get Frank's kids anything. They just received. They received what Frank's family wanted them to receive—love. My kids hadn't had their performance boulders fully developed like their dad's!

Hopefully, you are starting to see a couple things by now. First, this performance-based thinking runs deep. It starts from a very early age and impacts us in ways that we might not necessarily see, understand or realize. It doesn't just impact our relationship with God. It impacts all our relationships.

Secondly, you are hopefully starting to see that this type of thinking is a problem that needs addressing. As the above examples show, it skews life. It handicaps our ability to love and be loved. It prevents us from receiving unconditionally because our performance-based thinking requires us to put conditions on it. Performance-based thinking teaches us that we have to make things equal and measure ourselves against other people.

There are boulders underneath the surface and they are a problem. Let's start looking at how to address it. Again, we will turn to the Bible to see what God prescribes to address this. But first, spend some time to answer these questions.

WHAT ABOUT MY LIFE?

1. What situations do you find yourself trusting in your own experience and training?

2. What was your reaction to the statement that Bible reading and prayer don't bring us into God's presence? If you had a strong negative reaction, what do you think caused that?

3. Do feel like you are good at receiving from others? Do you have trouble receiving without giving anything in return? Do you find yourself trying to earn love from God and others?

CHAPTER 2

PERFORMANCE-BASED THINKING

TRANSFORM YOUR MIND

How do we approach fixing this performance-based problem? The Bible actually addresses performance-based thinking boulders. Let's look at another passage from the apostle Paul:

> Do not conform to the pattern of this world, but be transformed by the renewing of your mind. Then you will be able to test and approve what God's will is—his good, pleasing and perfect will. (Romans 12:2)

Here Paul talks about experiencing transformation in our lives. What does Paul say we need to do in order to be transformed? He instructs us to renew our minds and change our thinking. *We need to get rid of the old system of thinking based on ourselves and our behavior.*

Notice Paul does not say that we need to change ourselves to experience transformation. What we need to do is change our thinking. Nothing more.

God has made the necessary changes to our identity to experience new, transformed lives when we accept Jesus into our heart. We just *need to align our thinking to match* our new identities.

We read about our new identity as Christians in 2 Corinthians 5:17(ESV):

> Therefore, if anyone is in Christ, he is a new creation. The old has passed away; behold, the new has come.

When we accept Jesus into our lives, we are not improved versions of ourselves who still need work. The Bible says we are actually *NEW* creations. We are in a real sense "re-born." We are recreated to match God's original design and intent for our lives.

God did the hard part. He made a fundamental change to who we are. *Now our part is believing it. If we don't, our experience as Christians will never align with what God has done in us.*

Ultimately, performance-based thinking (PBT) is rooted in the world's thinking. We see this type of thinking supported by the media, schools and even our family and friends. This is the message that we get from society—we are valued by what we do and how others perceive us.

That's why Paul states in Romans 12:2 that we should not *"conform to the pattern of this world."* He wants us to break free from this way of thinking.

We get this type of message from school. The teacher doesn't say, "Well, you seem like a very nice girl, I'll give you an A." No, your value is linked to your performance. You are judged based on how well you do on papers and exams. You are categorized very early on and labeled as "smart" or "underachieving."

In elementary school we might be separated into the giraffe group or blue group, but everyone knows this is a high-achiever group or low-achiever group. Slowly but surely, this message starts to take root. We start deriving our value and identity from what we do and what we have accomplished.

The same type of thinking gets cultivated in the workplace. Your boss doesn't let you keep your job or get a raise because you are a child of God. They base it upon your performance. And it's not just your supervisor that is judging you and your performance, it's all your coworkers too.

Judgments about you and your performance are constantly being made. Whether it's to see if you are pulling your weight to meet a group goal or compare to their own performance, people are watching and making assessments of you.

We are constantly being judged on the basis of what we do and how we appear to others. As a result, our **PBT, performance-based thinking,** starts becoming more firmly established.

Sadly, this all starts in the home with our parents. Growing up we were judged based on our performance in the home and at school. Our performance is compared to our siblings or other relatives to see if we measure up.

"Did you hear that your cousin got into Harvard?" "Why can't you be like your sister (or brother)?" The implication? Who you are is not good enough. What you are doing is not good enough. You need to improve.

It may not be said overtly, but value is being attached to your performance and how others (family, neighbors, church friends, etc.) view your performance. PBT (performance-based thinking) is ingrained in us from a very early age and is subsequently reinforced over and over again as we enter school and then the workforce.

A GOOD REPORT?

Steve is a very successful man who grew up in a Christian home, but growing up, he never heard his parents say anything positive about him. He never received any kind of affirmation.

As an adult, he knew *intellectually* that his parents loved him even though they never outwardly expressed it or said it. They worked hard and sacrificed a lot for Steve and his sister. But as a child, Steve wasn't capable of thinking this objectively and *never felt loved by his parents.*

No matter what Steve did, it was never good enough. His dad in particular was never happy with anything that Steve did. Steve shared with me one incident in particular when he was in junior high.

It was the time of year when report cards were going to be mailed home. So, every day Steve rushed to check the mailbox. He wanted to beat his dad to the mail to intercept the report card.

Finally it came, and he nervously opened it up. He quickly looked at the report card. He had gotten 5 A's and a B! He was relieved, so he took it to his dad to sign.

This was more than twenty years ago, but Steve was still emotional sharing this next part. He went to give his dad the report card, and then he watched as his dad scanned it, looking at every grade. His dad looked up and said to Steve, "How come you got this B?"

Steve's earlier relief turned to shock. He thought, "Wow, are you kidding me? What about all those A's? Don't they count for anything? Didn't I do a good job in those classes?" But his dad's only comment was, "You've got to work harder."

Steve was devastated. He couldn't believe that his father had nothing good to say about all the A's he had gotten. The only thing his father focused on was his lone B. Something significant happened inside of him that day.

Looking back now, Steve can see how that event started forming and shaping his thinking. He could see how these words led him to start believing his value came from his performance because that's how his dad was judging him. Steve's PBT was forming.

Steve's acceptance was based upon his performance, therefore he started working really hard in school. He tried to be good at something that he knew his dad valued, so he could be affirmed by him. Because he was getting his value from what he did, it drove him to become a very good student.

Although the end result was good, the PBT was not. Steve now sees how he gets his value from his performance at work, at home and even at church. He is driven by people's expectations. He is not free. He sees how he is now passing this PBT to his own children.

Performance-based thinking is a faulty foundation that gets built from a very early age by everyone around us. It's this PBT that affected Steve growing up. It's this thinking that now affects Steve in all aspects of his life.

Can you relate to Steve? Can you see how PBT is like a virus that spreads and affects our daily life and relationships? It was certainly true for Steve.

ARE YOU WATCHING ME?

Performance-based thinking is so much a part of our life that the Bible frequently addresses it. Here are two examples I'd like you to consider. The first one comes from Jesus in Matthew 6:1-6:

> [1] "Be careful not to practice your righteousness in front of others to be seen by them. If you do, you will have no reward from your Father in heaven. [2] "So when you give to the needy, do not announce it with trumpets, as the hypocrites do in the synagogues and on the streets, to be honored by others. Truly I tell you, they have received their reward in full. [3] But when you give to the needy, do not let your left hand know what your right hand is doing, [4] so that your giving may be in secret. Then your Father, who sees what is done in secret, will reward you. [5] "And when you pray, do not be like the hypocrites, for they love to pray standing in the synagogues and on the street corners to be seen by others. Truly I tell you, they have received their reward in full. [6] But when you pray, go into your room, close the door and pray to your Father, who is unseen. Then your Father, who sees what is done in secret, will reward you.

Whenever I read this passage, it makes me reconsider anything I do in public. Should I read the Bible in public? What if people see me? Should I pray for my meal when I'm eating out? Am I praying so others can notice me praying?

But is this passage teaching us that we shouldn't do anything for God in front of others? I don't believe this was what Jesus was trying to convey. I believe He is addressing our tendency towards performance-based thinking.

Jesus is addressing the fact that we have a natural inclination towards wanting others to notice our actions. Jesus warns against believing our value comes from our performance and what others think.

When we are driven by wrong motives, Jesus says we have our reward in full (v. 5). We don't receive from Him. We just receive the fruit of our own doing. We don't receive the blessing that God intended, because we are being driven by our belief that our value and worth come from others and our performance. This is at the heart of PBT.

OH BROTHER, MY BROTHER

The second example comes from Genesis 4:3-8:

> [3] In the course of time Cain brought some of the fruits of the soil as an offering to the LORD. [4] And Abel also brought an offering—fat portions from some of the firstborn of his flock. The LORD looked with favor on Abel and his offering, [5] but on Cain and his offering he did not look with favor. So Cain was very angry, and his face was downcast. [6] Then the LORD said to Cain, "Why are you angry? Why is your face downcast? [7] If you do what is right, will you not be accepted? But if you do not do what is right, sin is crouching at your door; it desires to have you, but you must rule over it." [8] Now Cain said to his brother Abel, "Let's go out to the field." While they were in the field, Cain attacked his brother Abel and killed him.

We see from this passage that Cain and Abel brought their offerings to God. Abel's offering is regarded well by God, while Cain's was rejected. Verse 5 says that Cain became angry. How angry? We learn in v. 8 that Cain is so angry that he takes his brother into the field and kills him!

Is it just me or is that a bit of an overreaction? Cain gets his offering rejected. In v. 6 and 7, God tells Cain that this can be easily resolved by bringing a proper offering with the right motives. But instead, Cain goes out and kills his brother. Why is Cain's reaction so irrational and severe?

Well this makes no sense if it's simply about Cain's offering. Cain (like so many of us) was gaining his value from his performance and measuring up against his brother's performance. The comparison is clear. Cain's offering is being set up in contrast to Abel's offering.

Cain is so tied to his performance and measuring up to his brother, that when his offering is rejected, *he personally feels rejected.* To make matters worse, his brother's offering is accepted by God. Not only is Cain rejected, but his brother is a witness. Cain's value is diminished in his eyes, his brother's eyes and in the eyes of God (at least from Cain's perspective).

When we see that it's more than just his offering that is rejected, but Cain himself, we can begin to understand his violent reaction. We need to see that this story isn't simply about Cain's offering, but about things bubbling below the surface in Cain's thinking. Only then, can we make sense of the volcanic eruption within Cain that leads to the first homicide in human history!

From this account, we can start seeing the destructive effects of PBT. When we derive our value from our performance and what others think of us, we can also find ourselves overreacting like Cain. As a result, people in our lives can get injured.

THE TERRIBLE TWO'S

When God started pointing out my PBT, I noticed its effects in every aspect of my life. I began realizing that I was deriving my value from my performance and what others thought about me all the time. Let's look at a time when it affected me as a father.

My son was two years old when I took him shopping with me to Target. To be honest, I hate shopping. I like to get what I want and then leave with no detours. But on this day, my son had other plans.

When we got inside Target, he immediately took off running. He started to run towards the toy section. I tried to stop him by saying, "No, no, no! Come back here!" Undeterred, he kept trying to wander off, and so I pulled him towards me.

I was dragging him along saying, "No, we're going to go over here. We're getting this one thing and then we're going back home." He would have none of that. He started screaming and yelling.

All of the sudden he was on the floor of Target, face first on the ground. He had a full-blown tantrum (like only a two-year old can do) in the middle of Target!

As a parent I was thinking, "Oh, my goodness!" I felt like everybody in the whole store was looking at me wondering, "What is he going to do? He has no control over his son. What kind of parent is he?" It probably wasn't true, but I felt like all eyes were on me. Then something began to rise up within me.

I wish I could say it was love and compassion, but it was anger and impatience. I proceeded to pick up my son, who was kicking and screaming, and I carried him out of Target into the parking lot. I put him into the car and slammed the door.

Then, I just let him have it. I yelled at him and asked him "Why were you acting like that? Why were you trying to embarrass me?" Of course, my son did not answer. He just cried like a two-year old would when his father is berating him in the middle of the Target parking lot.

When I look back on my actions, I have to ask myself, "Why did I overreact like that?" He was only two years old. He didn't know what he was doing. He was not trying to set out to embarrass me. He was acting his age. But this didn't stop me from imploding and then exploding.

The question is where did that anger come from? Why was my reaction to that situation so over the top? *The intensity of emotions on the inside was not matching what was actually happening on the outside with my son.* It is clear that something else beyond my son's tantrum was at work. It was my PBT, performance-based thinking.

I was deriving my value from what other people were thinking about me. When my son was down there on the ground and everybody was looking at me, I could not handle it. Because I was finding my value so much from what other people thought about me, it caused me to lose control. I was getting upset, not so much because of what my son did, but from the emotions that were boiling inside me.

It was not the tantrum that caused my sinful reaction. I know this because this was not the first time my son had thrown a tantrum, but it had never happened in such a public way. When it happened in private, I was much more patient and understanding because there was no audience judging me.

Believe me, I would still feel frustration and get upset at his tantrums. But that day at Target was different. It was not the tantrum that I was reacting to on that day, it was the fireworks going off inside of me! I was overreacting because of the emotional tidal wave caused by my PBT.

It's very important that I made this realization. *If I hadn't, I would have thought that it was just about my circumstance. If I hadn't seen that there was a problem with my thinking that was causing the fireworks and my overreaction, I would have turned all my attention on my son and thought he was the problem.*

On that day it was my PBT that was the real problem. It was believing my value came from what others thought about me as a parent that was the source of my anger and overreaction. It wasn't my son.

If I kept thinking that it was my son, I would have never made strides to address the real issue. If I thought that it was my son that was the problem, all my focus would be on trying to fix him, instead of trying to address the real problem—my PBT. Should I have addressed my son's tantrums? Sure. *But the real issue was my sinful overreaction, not his behavior.*

When God revealed the truth of what was happening, my mind and heart were in a position to have Him address it. As God started to address my PBT, I started to see it change me as a parent. My interactions with my kids changed. It transformed me as a father. It transformed my kids and our relationship.

How many times has that happened to us as parents? How many times have we made it about our kids and not realized that the real issue was with our PBT? *How often have our kids been the victim of our anger or frustration coming from the boulder of PBT?*

If you are feeling the pain that comes from this type of thinking, that's a good thing. It's a good thing because you are seeing the seriousness of this problem and you are on the right path to address it.

MORE PBT REVELATIONS

Whenever I see a top ten list of things that people are afraid of, one thing is always at or near the top. If you were thinking it was the fear of public speaking, you'd be right. Sometimes it ranks higher than snakes, spiders and even the fear of death! Why?

When we are in the public-eye, something gets revealed. What gets revealed is our PBT. Our intense fear of public speaking comes from the fact that our performance and what others think about us gets amplified. When we are on stage, we can sense that all eyes are on us. People are judging us. They are evaluating us.

We imagine people are thinking things like, "This person doesn't know what they are talking about. Why do they keep hemming and hawing? Why do they keep putting their hand in their pocket? Why do they look so flustered up there?"

All of these are things I've thought. It's no surprise when I became a pastor that delivering the message on Sunday in front of a church audience became a huge source of stress.

Early on in my ministry, I would get very anxious before I would preach. I began to worry what people were going to think about me. Were they going to wonder if I knew what I was talking about or if I was too young to be teaching them (I started out at 28 years old)?

When I first started out, I didn't have to speak that often. Yet even though I didn't speak regularly, it didn't prevent me from worrying and stressing out. I was so anxious about it that I started to work on my message weeks ahead of time.

Even so, the week before I was scheduled to speak, I would try to clear my calendar. I didn't need that time to prepare. I would have spent weeks going over the message, but I wouldn't schedule anything because I was so nervous.

After a few months of this, my wife started to recognize this pattern. She knew what I was like before I would have my turn to preach, so she would try to give me space. She steered clear of me because I was not pleasant to be around!

Why was I like that? Why was I anxious when I was so well-prepared? Why did my stress level get so high that I couldn't engage in other activities or with other people, even my family?

The answer was PBT. So much of my value came from my performance and what others thought about me that it caused me to overreact every time it was my turn to preach. My anxiety stemmed from fear. I was that afraid of what people were going to think about me as a pastor and as a speaker. I was afraid I wasn't going to live up to their expectations.

It wasn't the preaching that was the problem. I did, and do, enjoy the actual preaching. I love teaching. I love encouraging. I feel like it's part of who God made me to be. But my PBT caused so much anxiousness within me that I could never fully enjoy it. PBT stripped the life and enjoyment from something God created me to do.

MY THREE-POINT PRAYER

This performance-based thinking was so ingrained that it would even affect me when I was praying for someone. At church I would sense God leading me to pray for a person. Then, I would need to pause and pray. Pray for myself!

I would think, "OK, I better pray an awesome prayer because I'm the pastor. The pastor has to have an extraordinary prayer. I better bless this person's socks off!" That's what I would think, which created all this pressure.

As a result, I would try to think and plan out my prayer beforehand. I would say to myself, "Maybe I'll pray this first, then I will pray that. And oh yeah, then I'll close with this." It's like I was preparing to deliver a three-point message.

When I look back at what I was doing, it makes me sad. I'm sad because I left no room for God to come and bless the person. *It was all coming from me. It was all coming from my flesh, my own doing, thinking and trying.*

I left no room for God's Spirit to come, touch the person and give them what they really needed, which was to hear from Him. I needed to hear from Him too. But my PBT left no room for that.

Since I believed my worth came from what people thought about me as a pastor, that effectively squeezed God out of the equation. Because I was so concerned about what they'd think of me, I used my own wisdom instead of letting God take control.

I couldn't just let God use me. I couldn't trust God to dictate the prayer. I had to dictate the prayer. I had to be in control because of my fear and insecurity. All this was the result of getting my value from my performance and what others thought.

Can you relate? How about you in your workplace? Can you see your PBT affecting you? Can you see its effects with your boss or coworkers? Does PBT crowd God out of your workplace? It did for me and I work for a church!

Just to show how widespread this PBT epidemic was in my own life, let me give you one more example. Growing up I never had a pet of any kind. I had a fish from a carnival that lived a couple of days, but that was the extent of my pet ownership.

Then one day my kids started begging me to get a dog. At first, I was strong. But eventually they wore me down and we ended up getting a little puppy. We named her Coco.

After getting Coco, I wanted to be a good, faithful dog owner. I enrolled the two of us in a dog obedience class. I thought it was a good plan, but I had no idea what to expect. We went to this class with all these other dogs and their owners. The instructor taught us how to get our dog to come, lie down, and roll over. It was actually fun.

I was really enjoying my time in this class. I was going week after week and learning all these different tricks to do with my dog. Then something happened. It was week five of this eight-week course and the instructor started saying that we needed to practice at home.

I wasn't worried because I was already practicing at home. Then she continued, "You need to practice at home because in a few weeks, we're going to have a test." What? A test? I did not sign up for a test. All of a sudden my experience totally changed. I began feeling all this pressure.

What are the other dog owners going to think about me if my dog can't do all these tricks? I started to feel anxious about this test that was coming, so I stepped it up. I started practicing more at home, way more. But now, when my little pup was not listening, I became more and more impatient.

Before it was no big deal if she wouldn't come or lie down, but now the stakes were raised! I noticed I was getting more frustrated when she was unable or unwilling to do the tricks. *I wasn't enjoying things like I was before.*

Fast forward to week eight. Three days before the test, I took Coco for a walk down a particularly busy street in our neighborhood. We stopped to wait at a light so that we could cross the street. Cars were flying by.

While we waited on the corner, Coco, being a little pup, started getting impatient for the light to change. Suddenly she wrapped herself around the light pole and the leash disconnected from her collar. When it came loose, my dog ran straight into the street.

I remember the next seconds happened in slow motion. I reached out, but I couldn't stop her. Then a car came whooshing by and hit Coco. My dog is tiny. She is ten pounds soaking wet. So when she got hit, I was thinking the worst. She started screeching, as she was lying there in the middle of the street. I was thinking this might be the end.

Then a lady who was also waiting at the light shouted over to me. She had seen what happened and offered to give us a ride to the vet. I accepted.

At the vet, I explained what had happened. They told me that they would look at her and take some x-rays. After they finished, they would get back to me. The whole time the vet didn't look too optimistic. I left Coco at the vet and went back home.

I thought about how I was going to break the news to my kids. I told them about our dog getting hit by a car and they started to cry. I told them not to worry, even though I was very worried. Then the vet called to let us know the x-rays were done and wanted us to come in.

I went in prepared to hear the bad news when suddenly the vet declared, "There is nothing here on the x-rays. There's no fracture. Nothing!" I was dumbfounded. God miraculously saved my dog. This little tiny dog survived this collision with a car going 50 mph!

Want to know the very next thought that ran through my mind? "This dog is going to fail the test!" This is how messed up my thinking was. My dog miraculously survived a life-threatening accident and I was worried she was going to fail the dog obedience test on Saturday!

On Saturday morning I got to class early. In the parking lot, I put all the seats down in the back of my minivan. Then I went to the back of the car with Coco to practice all the commands. She wasn't doing any of them, not one. My worst fears were realized. She was still traumatized by her accident and she was not going to pass this test.

I went inside to get it over with. During the test, they took the dogs one by one into a separate room. The owners had to sit in a waiting room while they took their dogs to get tested. After they finished, they gathered everyone together to get the results.

I readied myself to hear that she had failed, when the instructor tells the group that Coco was the only dog who had passed! When it was game time, my dog came through! God certainly has a sense of humor!

This humorous story shows how PBT affects even the smallest areas of our lives. Insignificant things like a dog obedience test are not exempt. Getting our value from our performance and what other people think about us can affect us on a daily basis. But this is not what God intended for us.

God didn't intend for us to have this type of experience or way of thinking. This is not the foundation He wanted us to build our life upon. He wants us to have a secure foundation built on Christ, not on ourselves.

We need to make that transition. We need to renew our minds. We need to shift our thinking so we can break free of the hold PBT has on our lives. When we do, everything will change.

This happened with me when I began shifting my thinking. My life turned upside down (in a good way). The rest of this book will chronicle my journey to freedom and examples from others who have experienced this same shift.

WHAT ABOUT MY LIFE?

1. Did you connect with any of the stories in this chapter? How has PBT affected you as a parent, student, in the workplace, as a dog owner, or other areas?

2. How would things change if you didn't get your value from your performance or what others thought about you?

JOURNEY TO **FREEDOM**

How do we break free from this pattern of thinking that's plagued us for our entire lives? On this journey, there are three phases we will navigate through that will take us from performance-based thinking to freedom.

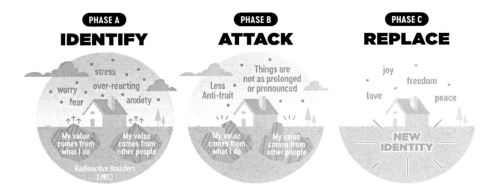

PHASE A – IDENTIFY
During Phase A, we will learn to recognize the signs and symptoms of PBT. It is important to understand these signs and symptoms and how they can help us in identifying our performance-based thinking.

PHASE B – ATTACK
During this phase, I will introduce two tools to attack our PBT. First, we can directly counteract this type of thinking by understanding and practicing true repentance to receive God's forgiveness and love unconditionally. Second, we will learn about a Reflection Tool that can be used to defuse the power this type of thinking has over our lives.

PHASE C – REPLACE
In the third and final phase, we will look to replace PBT with a new way of approaching our performance. We will examine what our post-PBT life can look like. Lastly, we will paint a picture of *ultimate* freedom and how we experience more of it in our lives.

CHAPTER 3

PHASE A: IDENTIFY PBT

Now that we're beginning to understand the problem with performance-based thinking (PBT), how do we identify when the problem manifests in our own lives? Let's revisit the house analogy from Chapter 1.

Remember the radioactive boulders that caused the homeowner to be sick? Those radioactive boulders represented our PBT: deriving our value from our performance and getting our value from others' view of us. When we carry this radioactive thinking (below the surface) for an extended period of time, it will naturally start showing up in everyday life (above ground).

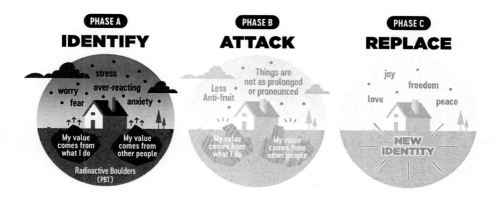

When we look at the diagram, we can see the two radioactive PBT boulders below ground. Above ground we see the radioactive dust that this type of thinking has produced. This dust clouds our ability to see things clearly.

I call this radioactive dust: <u>**anti-fruit**</u>. The prefix "anti" means opposed to or against. Anti-fruit is a term that I use to describe the negative result of living life contrary to what God desires for us.

Anti-fruit manifests in our lives as overreacting, stress, anxiety, fear, anger, and insecurity. This is the byproduct of getting our identity and value from ourselves (and others) apart from God. Since this is not how God designed us, it makes sense that we'd start seeing the negative effects in our lives.

God never designed us to earn our value from what we do and what others think about us. When we continue to operate outside of God's design, it will eventually produce this negative fruit. Stress and the other radioactive material are the natural outflow from living with this performance-based thinking.

When we continue deriving our value from our performance and what others think, we'll be living life on a shaky foundation that God never intended for us. As a result, that's why we feel so insecure. That's why we experience so much anti-fruit and so little of the freedom and joy God wants us to experience.

ANTI-FRUIT CAN HELP

We are so used to thinking our value and identity come from these two PBT boulders that it seems normal. There's no alarm or flag that goes off in our minds signaling us that we have a problem. On a day-to-day basis, we may never realize that these PBT boulders are looming below the surface, *but* we are well aware of the effects above ground.

Whereas we might have difficulty noticing the PBT in our lives, it's very easy to recognize the anti-fruit. It takes very little effort to recognize the stress, impatience, anger, and other anti-fruit. Anti-fruit is abundant, and we *know* it's a problem.

However, we can actually *use the anti-fruit to help us.* Stress and other anti-fruit can help identify where the PBT shows up in our lives. Since anti-fruit is a result of performance-based thinking, when we experience the anti-fruit, it can help signal when PBT is at work.

This is the goal of Phase A: identify when we are influenced by our PBT. When we are able to identify the boulders, then we can direct our efforts in removing them (Phase B).

But in order for anti-fruit to help us identify where PBT is showing up, we need to be convinced that it's the *radioactive thinking that's the real problem and not the anti-fruit.* It's natural for us to believe that stress, impatience and other anti-fruit is the real issue we need to deal with and not PBT.

SYMPTOM MANAGEMENT

We don't need convincing that anti-fruit is a problem. *But we have to see that it's really a symptom and not the source of our problems.* It is not always easy to recognize the distinction. Often, we see the anti-fruit as THE problem we are facing. We see anger and think that's what we need to tackle. We see stress and believe that is the *main* issue.

If I had a runny nose and kept on trying to address it directly I would plug my nose with tissue. I would put vapor rub under my nostrils. I would do these things thinking I'm solving the problem. But what I'm actually doing is just trying to manage the symptoms.

This is the way we've learned to handle the anti-fruit in our lives. It is through symptom management. Let's look at an example. We will take one of the most common anti-fruit, stress.

When things in our lives are not going well and we face difficulties over an extended period of time, it produces stress in our lives. When we experience stress, which has become so commonplace, how do we respond?

In my experience with hundreds of people, the most common way people try to tackle the problem is through stress management. They try to handle the stress by managing it through getting more rest, taking a vacation, saying "no" more often, developing boundaries, eating better, exercising more, sleeping more, and maybe even some spiritual things like praying!

But there is a problem here. Do you see it? The way we are trying to tackle our stress is to *manage* it. Still don't see the problem? *What we are doing is trying to manage the symptoms. We are not trying to deal with what is causing the stress.* We are not trying to explore the root of the problem.

Instead, we are almost conceding that stress will be a part of our lives and the best we can do is to try and minimize its effects. That's why I don't even like the term stress management. It starts off conceding defeat. It assumes that we will always have stress, so let's focus our efforts on trying to minimize or manage it. I don't want to manage it. I want to eliminate it!

The problem develops because stress may seem like an unavoidable part of life. It often seems normal. Can we really have a life with no stress, no anxiety, or no worry? Let's see what our good friend Paul has to say on the subject. He writes about this in Philippians 4:6:

> Do not be anxious about anything, but in every situation, by prayer
> and petition, with thanksgiving, present your requests to God.

When Paul writes that "we are not to be anxious about anything," he means we are not to be anxious about ANY-THING. Not just about the necessities of life. Not just about the really big things. Nothing.

He doesn't leave a lot of wiggle room here, does he? We are not to be anxious or stressed out about anything in our lives. Instead, we are to bring those stressors to our Heavenly Father, who cares for us.

Sounds good, but is that realistic? Are we really supposed to have no anxiety in our lives? What was Paul thinking? Why did he give this command?

I'M SINNING ALL THE TIME

A person I was mentoring asked me a question while we were studying Philippians 4:6. He asked, "if Paul is instructing us to not be anxious, would stress be a sin?" I responded that if Paul is giving this as a command and we don't obey it, then yes, it is sin.

He had a shocked look on his face and said, "Well, I'm sinning all the time then!" I can completely relate to his sentiment. Can being stressed and anxious be a sin? It seems like a normal part of our lives. *But this is where we need to fall back on the truth of the Bible, not in our ability to experience its truth.*

The Bible is unambiguous. We are to not worry or be anxious. This is God's intent and design for us. We can't let go of that truth, even if we can't see how that's possible. However, we are going to find out that *it is possible.*

Is it possible that we are *never* going to stress again? No, I'm not saying that. But what I am saying is that we can start having more times and seasons when we are not experiencing anxiety or stress. We can experience more of the worry-free living that God intended for us.

The first step? No more symptom management. No more stress management. No more trying through our own effort to improve our capacity to handle stress. No more conceding that we will always have stress.

No more thinking that stress is normal. It's not normal. It's not what God prescribed for his people as the norm. If it was, why would Paul give the command to not do it?

The next step is to redirect our efforts. Instead of pouring so much effort into trying to minimize the stress through working harder or smarter, we need to direct it towards the source. If we try to just manage the symptoms (the anti-fruit) without addressing the source (what's producing it), we'll find ourselves having to manage it for the rest of our lives!

RE-ROUTING THE SIGNAL

We can't let ourselves be consumed with dealing with the anti-fruit, instead of the source. Or . . . *maybe our stress management is our attempt to kill the root.* Perhaps we have been led to believe that the way to address the root of our stress *is* stress management.

But if that's the case, we need to see that it doesn't work! We need to see that this old way of handling things isn't effective. No matter how much we try to take a break from things, get more organized or work smarter, we will still have stress in our lives.

It may work for a day, a week or maybe even for a couple months. But eventually it creeps back into our lives. We need to see that being overworked is not the true source of stress and anxiousness.

Now I'm **not** saying that our workload doesn't produce any stress in our lives. It does. But long term, this is not the solution to eliminating stress. We have to see that how much we are doing is part of the problem. *But the main problem is not how much we are doing; it's how that work is affecting us.*

Because we derive our value so much from our performance and what others are thinking about us, it makes our workload feel a hundred times heavier. The pressure, both internal and external, makes our work that much more difficult and . . . stressful!

THE 150-LB. BACKPACK

Trying to work while carrying all these expectations is like trying to live life with a 150-lb. backpack on. We need to see that this backpack full of performance-based boulders is the *main* source of our strain and stress.

Imagine if you could take off that 150-lb. backpack. Imagine how much easier it would be to walk around and get things done. How different would your experience be if you didn't get your value from your performance and the results you are producing? How freeing it would be to not get your value and identity from what other people are saying or thinking about you.

If you don't remove this 150-lb. backpack, then reducing your workload won't be as effective. It won't be as effective because you are still carrying the weight of expectations, measuring up and failures. *What good is reducing your workload, when we are still carrying all that stress producing weight?*

On the flip side, if you do take off the backpack and then try to reduce your workload, you will see results. However, you might find that reducing your load is unnecessary. Once you remove that extra weight you've been carrying on your shoulders, you might find that you no longer feel overloaded.

What I've found is that once people take off the backpack, many no longer have the sense that they are doing too much. They actually feel like they can take on more!

We need to recognize that trying to manage anti-fruit is not effective. It may give some temporary relief, but it will have no lasting effects. We need to address the real problem—the 150-lb. backpack that's filled with two gigantic boulders of performance and other people's judgment and expectations.

We need to re-route the signal. We need anti-fruit to signal us to address PBT in our lives, not to manage symptoms. When we experience stress, we need that to direct us to address the boulders, not try to reduce our workload. Remember, we can address the workload, but *after* we remove the backpack, *not instead* of removing it!

God can redeem even the negative anti-fruit in our lives. He can and will use all of our failures and missteps for our good. Isn't that just like God to turn something negative (like stress) into something positive (identify performance-based thinking)? We read about this truth in Romans 8:28:

> And we know that in all things God works for the good of those who love him, who have been called according to his purpose.

WHAT ABOUT MY LIFE?

1. What anti-fruit is prominent in your life? What situations or relationships often produce that anti-fruit?

2. What steps have you tried to manage anti-fruit symptoms? Has it been successful?

3. Take a moment to imagine what it would be like to take off the 150-pound backpack full of trying to measure up, proving yourself to others, and feeling the pressure to perform. (Note: this is the life that God intends for us)

CHAPTER 4

ROAD SIGNS

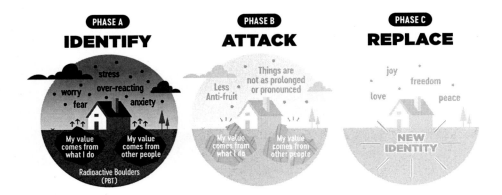

During Phase A, we need to use the negative anti-fruit in our lives to shine a light on our radioactive, PBT boulders. As we move along this road to freedom, let's look at two anti-fruit road signs that will help us to identify when we're dealing with a performance boulder.

These road signs are common anti-fruit that appear when we get our value from our performance and what others are thinking about us. After introducing the road signs, we will look at a few examples of how these signs show up in our lives.

ROAD SIGN #1: GUILT AND OBLIGATION

When we get our value from our performance and ability, we are going to experience guilt and obligation. This pair of anti-fruit is one road sign that we will encounter when dealing with these boulders. When this anti-fruit pops up, a caution flag needs to rise up and tell us to look more closely at our performance-based thinking.

When we place so much value on what we do, it's natural that we will be carrying an inordinate amount of guilt and obligation. We carry this guilt and obligation from not measuring up, sin, failure and needing to compensate others for what they've done. In a moment we will look at some real-life examples, but first let's look at a second pair of rotten anti-fruit that comes from these boulders.

ROAD SIGN #2: INSECURITY AND FEAR

A second road sign that shows up when we face the PBT boulders is insecurity and fear. If we are deriving our value from our performance, more than likely it's going to produce these two, not so wonderful anti-fruit.

The reason? God never intended us to get our sense of security and identity from our performance and others' view of us. When we place our trust in what we do, we'll feel unstable. We will feel insecure because we have a shaky foundation. As long as we are leaning on this faulty foundation, we will *never* feel safe and secure.

God doesn't want us to build our foundation on this shaky ground of our own doing. He wants us to build it on the rock, upon Jesus (see Matthew 7:24-27). When we build our house on the sand, it shouldn't be a surprise that we feel insecure and fearful. When our foundation is faulty, it doesn't take much for the wind to shake our house (or knock it down!).

ALL THAT GLITTERS IS NOT GOLD

One compelling example comes from when we look at the most talented people in society. Take a look at the people who are the most gifted in music, sports or entertainment.

These are people at the highest peak. They are on top of their professional mountains. They are people who are the most successful, most attractive, strongest or most athletic. But when you look at some of these people, you will see they are often extremely insecure.

You might ask, "What reason do they have to be insecure?" They are at the top of their profession. They are so talented and attractive. What do they have to be insecure about? Well strangely enough, their insecurity stems from the fact that they are so talented or attractive. Let me explain.

Since they are really good at something (and have everyone telling them how good they are), they most likely have spent their entire lives getting their value from their performance and what others think of them. *Because they are so good at what they do, they naturally begin to attach their value to their performance.* They begin building their PBT boulders from a very early age.

Their whole life they've had people telling them, "You are so great, you are awesome. Look at how beautiful you are." It's ironic because we think that this should make them feel more secure, not less. And in the short term, they will feel secure, like nothing is wrong.

But when a trial or emptiness hits, they will realize that their foundation is not secure. They sense the unsettledness inside. They recognize the lack of peace and fulfillment. You see many turn to drugs or alcohol to fill the void. You see their insecurity as they jump from one relationship to the next. You see it as they grasp for other things to fill the void.

This is not the secure foundation that God wants us to build on. He doesn't want us to build on a foundation that is based upon our performance and others' view of us. And when we do, we will feel the negative effects.

We can learn an important lesson when we see these incredibly talented people. We can see that building our trust in our ability doesn't produce security. Since that's not how God designed us, we will not become more secure through our own work and successes.

Sometimes we look at these people and wish that we could be more like them. The thinking is that if we were as talented or powerful as they are, we would be better off. If we were more like them, we wouldn't be so insecure and fearful. But this is a facade.

EVERYBODY LOVES AMANDA

Meet Amanda. She is very popular. She was a homecoming queen. She has tons of friends. Everyone loves Amanda. But Amanda is also insecure (road sign to a boulder).

She is so insecure that she struggles with anxiety and depression. Her parents were worried about her. She hadn't been able to go to school for weeks. They took her to a psychologist. But they'd seen no change.

Amanda's mom asked me to talk with her. I met with Amanda and her mom. Amanda confessed that she was very nervous but was open to meeting with me. I talked to Amanda about what she thought might be the source of her depression.

She said that she was constantly worried that no one liked her. This was shocking for me to hear because I didn't know a single person who didn't like Amanda. She went on to say that she did everything that she could to get people to like her, but it was not working.

She told me that her psychologist tried to show her the evidence that this was not true. He showed her letters from her peers telling Amanda that they thought the world of her (her mom helped gather these). It made no difference. Amanda reasoned, "What else are they going to say when you ask them to write these letters?"

I realized that this was not the right route. They could have lined up a whole host of witnesses testifying that they adored her, but she would still be insecure and severely so. Amanda was standing on a fault line. This was shaky ground.

Since Amanda was so talented and popular, she had always gotten her value from what others had said about her. It became normal. From her parents to her aunts and uncles to her friends, everybody had been singing her praises.

From a very early age, her boulder began forming. It was not surprising that insecurity soon followed. In Amanda's case, the insecurity led to anxiety and depression. Everyone was baffled as to why she would be depressed since everyone liked her and she was so gifted and talented. It didn't make any sense.

On the surface, her situation doesn't make sense, until you look below the surface where we see the source of her insecurity and fear. It was her performance-based thinking that had developed over her entire life that was causing her to experience this anti-fruit.

Now, let's be clear. *It wasn't the fact that she was talented and gifted that made her insecure. It was that she derived her value and identity from it that put her on shaky ground.* There are many talented and gifted people who do not get their value from what they do. Those people are often very secure.

However, with Amanda, this is how she had gotten her sense of value her whole life. It had worked when she was little, but now the cracks were showing. No matter how hard she tried, she couldn't feel secure.

We can learn a lot from her story. We can see that insecurity doesn't have to come from an inability but sometimes find its root from being very capable. It's an easy trap to fall into.

Do well. Get praised. Do your best to do it again and maybe better than before. Get praised even more. Get your value and identity from your performance. Do fine, until the storms of life hit to reveal a faulty foundation.

THE PRODIGAL PARTY POOPER

I don't know if you have it titled this way in your Bible, but this is a story of the "prodigal party pooper." Ok, maybe that's just my version. We find this story in Luke 15:11-32. Let me summarize:

It begins with a father who has two sons. The younger son decides that he wants his inheritance now even though his father is not dead yet. This certainly says something about what he thinks about his father.

According to Jewish custom, the eldest son would receive twice as much of the father's inheritance as the other sons. In this case, the younger son would be due one-third and the older son two-thirds of the family estate. The younger son wants his one-third now.

The father *graciously* gives his younger son his inheritance. The son takes it and spends it on wild living. He spends it on prostitutes (Luke 15:30). He spends it on partying and worldly pleasures.

Then he runs out of money.

He has spent all of his father's hard-earned money. He is hungry with no resources in the middle of a famine. He gets a menial job tending pigs.

He is sitting there with the pigs (for a Jew this is rock bottom) thinking "What am I doing here? I'd be much better off just being a servant at my father's house." He decides to go back to his father's house, but not without a plan.

He maps out what he's going to say to his father. After some deliberation, he comes up with this: "Dad, I know that I'm not worthy to be called your son. I'm not even worthy to be one of your hired servants, *please* take me back."

Now the camera pans to his father. The father is waiting for his son. He is literally waiting and watching for his return. It's at this point he sees his son from a distance.

What does the father do? He starts running over to his son. This is very unexpected for a Jewish father, but he is so overcome with joy that he races off.

Then *before* the son gets to deliver his speech, the father embraces him and hugs him. Before the son gets to employ his plan, before he says anything to him, the father welcomes and receives him.

The son *doesn't understand what's going on,* so he spits out his pre-planned apology anyway. But that's when the father tells his servants, "Bring the robe and a ring and the fattened calf," and decides to have a party for his son.

This is where I'd like to press pause on the story in order to put ourselves in the sandals of this young man. What would you be thinking at this point? You've basically told your father that you consider him dead. You take his life savings and spend it on things that would make your father's skin crawl. Now he's embracing you and throwing you a party!

Imagine yourself at this party. What are you feeling? You've come crawling back home with your tail between your legs ready to beg for forgiveness and be a hired hand. Now you are at this celebration thrown in your honor. Your honor! How ironic is that? Do you have any honor?

Are you having fun at this party? What are all the servants thinking about you? They all know what you've done. Then you notice your older brother, who was faithful to your father, is not there. You can only imagine what your older brother is thinking about you. While you were gone, his burden increased exponentially because you were so irresponsible.

All your friends are there too (see Luke 15:29). They also know what you've done. Maybe some of those friends were the ones who partied with you. And then the father kills the fattened calf (the best of the lot) that is reserved for special occasions for you and your guests.

Wow. What are you feeling now? Happy, nervous, unworthy? Are you feeling divided and conflicted? Do you really want to be there? Do you really want your old friends there?

Now, I want you to consider what you think the father *wants* you to be feeling. Why does he throw this party in the first place? What does he want you to experience?

It's clear. He would want you to feel loved and accepted. He wants you to feel the love that is pouring out of his heart. The party is dripping wet with his *unconditional* love for you.

Yet what you are feeling? Guilty? Ashamed? Embarrassed? Sad? Regretful? Unworthy? Sick? A sense of obligation? Feeling the need to make up for your wrongdoing? If you are like me, it's all of the above.

But loved? Joyful? Not so much. But why not? *If the father wants us to feel loved, why are we feeling anything but loved?* There is a disconnect here.

What we are thinking and feeling at the party is not matching what the father, who represents God, wants us to experience. God is expressing His heart for us, but we are not receiving it. Again, we have to ask the question, "Why?"

It's guilt and obligation. It's our PBT, performance-based thinking. It's thinking we don't deserve this. We can't receive this because we don't merit it. Not only do we not deserve a party, but we deserve punishment. *This performance-based thinking disqualifies us from receiving what God wants to give us.*

How many of us are hungry for God's love? How long have we been thirsting for more acceptance? Not just in our head, but in our heart. Not something we *only* read about in the Bible, but a genuine sense that He loves and accepts us. We long to feel His heart and overwhelming joy for us.

We need to recognize that our PBT is the hindrance. It handicaps us when we try to sense and experience God's love for us. It's our performance thinking that precludes us from receiving from Him.

As we see in this story, the bottleneck is not the Father. He is running to us. He wants to throw us a party because He loves being with us that much. He wants to use the fattened calf reserved for only the most special occasions because this is how He feels about us. No, the bottleneck is not the Father.

The bottleneck is us and our wrong thinking. It's our thinking that changes our perception. It's our thinking that is the blockage. *Feeling love, joy and the Father's heart for us is not on our radar when we sin.* It's not within the realm of possibility when we fail or do things that hurt our Heavenly Father.

That's why instead of feeling loved, we feel guilt (road sign). That's why instead of feeling joy, we feel shame. That's why instead of feeling the heart of the Father for us, we feel rejected. We do it to ourselves.

It's not the Father's love that is in question here. It's our ability to receive it that is the problem. It's our thinking that if our actions don't measure up, we cannot and should not be receiving love from God. We have to realize our inability to receive stems from our PBT and the faulty foundation that we've built.

We have to let guilt and obligation signal us. We have to hit the brakes when we see this roadblock. Performance-based thinking is blocking us from receiving what our Father wants to give us and has already given us.

WHAT ABOUT MY LIFE?

1. Do you often struggle with a sense of guilt and insecurity? In what situations or relationships do you find yourself feeling this way?

2. Think about the prodigal son story recounted in this chapter. What are all the feelings, thoughts and emotions you would have been experiencing at your welcome home party. Could you see yourself actually enjoying the party, as your father intended?

CHAPTER 5

PULLING BACK THE VEIL

Last chapter we revealed two helpful road signs or anti-fruit that will help us in Phase A of this journey to freedom (identifying PBT). As we look at this next story, we'll see how one of these road signs helped me identify and address my PBT boulder. I pray that as you read this the Holy Spirit will pull back the veil so you can see the boulders in your own life.

THREE-RING CIRCUS, PART II

Remember the three-ring circus that described the early years of my marriage? We were struggling as a newly married couple. We continually came across the same problems and arguments.

They say the definition of insanity is doing the same thing over and over and expecting a different result. We both felt a little insane during this time. We were coming across the same pattern hoping that things would be different the next time.

One night, things got really out of hand. We had a serious blow up. We argued and fought well into the night. We were both tired but we kept on arguing.

If I was honest, it was often me driving the marathon sessions of endless arguing. You see, I couldn't handle it that my wife was upset with me and so I couldn't take my foot off the gas pedal until everything was ok again. This was one of those nights.

As we both grew more and more exhausted, our words came out sharper and more pointed. I said things to her that I wouldn't have said to my worst enemy. She had enough. She packed a bag and left. She spent the night at a hotel. She couldn't handle the fighting and hurtful words any longer. She wanted the pain to stop.

Even though she returned the next day, I had hit rock bottom. I was desperate. I would have done anything to change our marriage. This was the woman I loved and wanted to spend the rest of my life with. Yet our marriage was on shaky ground. I knew something had to change. I didn't realize that what had to change was ME.

After hitting our low point, God revealed what the real issue was. It started with recognizing my insecurity and fear (the second road sign). I noticed that my insecurity and fear were so strong that I couldn't address any issues that my wife brought up. It caused me to be defensive, angry and impatient.

However, that was not the real problem. Insecurity and fear were just the symptoms. So were the anger and defensiveness. Until God helped me see the connection between my anti-fruit and my radioactive, performance-based boulder, I was caught in the same cycle that kept repeating.

I tried to work on my anger or impatience, but it never stuck. It never worked because it wasn't the source of the problem. The root of our problems and arguments was me and my wrong thinking. *I found so much of my value and identity from what my wife thought about me that I couldn't receive any criticism.* As a result, I couldn't handle anything negative my wife said even if she communicated it gently.

Having built my house on the sand, a shaky foundation, made me feel insecure. I didn't feel like a secure child of God. I felt like an orphan. Getting my value from my wife and what she thought of me, instead of from God, produced this fearful, defensive and defenseless person.

My PBT was the source of our arguments. This is what caused them to escalate. This was the root of the cycle that developed. But as humbling as it was, it provided hope.

You see, all this time we were at a loss. We tried on our own to fix these problems. We tried with all our strength and effort to not get into these arguments.

We read books. We talked with other Christians. We tried everything we could think of. Some of these things helped, but it didn't take long for the pattern to return. When it did, we felt like we were at ground zero again.

After so much time and effort in trying to identify what the problem was, I was finally able to pinpoint it. And after thinking that my wife might be the problem, I realized I was wrong. It was me. It was my performance-based thinking. It was the boulder's radioactivity clouding my thinking and perception.

With all the radioactive anti-fruit, I couldn't receive any criticism from her. I couldn't address the actual issues that she brought up because the fireworks going off inside were too loud. It hurt too much. I couldn't see things objectively. I couldn't see if what she was saying was actually true.

To be honest, I didn't care if it was true or not. I was in survival mode. I put up my defenses. Some people respond by retreating to deal with the pain. I tried to fight back. I tried to turn the spotlight on her. I tried to take the spotlight off of myself.

Even though I often didn't have an issue with my wife, I made it about her anyway. I had to. I had to do something to address the insecurity. I had to cover up the hurt I was experiencing. I had to do something to try to make it stop.

The tragic thing is that my efforts to defuse my pain actually caused more pain. By trying to turn the tables and fight back, it led to my saying hurtful things to my wife. I ended up making a bad situation worse. Not only was I hurting, but now I found myself hurting the one whom I loved.

Ironically, I hurt the very person whose opinion I valued the most. This all stemmed from building my foundation on the sand. All this insecurity and fear came from deriving my value from another person and not from God. God never intended my house to stand on the opinions of other people, not even my spouse.

Now, I'm not saying that her opinion is not important. What she thinks is very important and plays a vital role in my life. But God never intended my *value and identity* to be grounded in her view of me.

God never designed her to have that sort of power. *Only God has the power and authority to determine someone's value and identity. Others can reinforce what God has done in creating you, but they cannot and should not replace Him*!

Insecurity and fear. God used this anti-fruit as a road sign pointing to the real problem. The real issue wasn't trying to accept the other person. It wasn't saying things nicer or being more sensitive. It wasn't counting to ten before responding. It wasn't any of these things. It was my radioactive boulder. It was trying to find my value from my wife instead of from God.

God used this terrible anti-fruit in my life to be a signal. It helped me to step into Phase A on the journey to freedom: Identify my PBT. This led to my marriage being radically changed. It led to me being transformed and my marriage hasn't been the same since.

I experienced freedom! Freedom to love. Freedom to connect. Freedom to hear from my wife. Freedom for her to express her heart to me. Freedom for our kids to feel more safe and secure in our home.

Now, do we still argue? Sure, but the frequency and intensity has been dialed back, way back. With the radioactive dust cleared, my perspective has changed. Now I can look more objectively at the things she brings up and see if it's really true. And if it is true, I want to receive it. This would have never happened before.

Once I recognized the problem, what did I do to overcome this boulder? How did we break this cycle? How did God change the momentum of our marriage? How did God transform me and eventually my family? What did I do to unlock this breakthrough? Well, you'll have to wait! I know, I'm cruel. But we will revisit this soon.

The important part right now is the recognition. Recognizing how my PBT wreaked havoc in my marriage. It created insecurity and fear in me. It made me incapable of having true, vulnerable connection with my wife.

Can you see how easy it is to see the anti-fruit as the problem? Can you see how tempting it is to address the symptoms? Working to build patience. Trying to control anger. Reading books on controlling your words.

Can you see how important it is to make the connection between the anti-fruit (insecurity and fear) and the real source of the problem, performance-based thinking? If I didn't recognize it, I would still be trying to manage the symptoms.

Addressing our PBT starts with Phase A and identifying the problem. If we can't see how performance-based thinking shows up in our lives, we will never be able to address it. *You cannot address what you cannot see.*

Are you starting to recognize how critical it is to *identify the PBT* in our lives? Its impact is far-reaching. PBT affects the most important people and relationships in our lives.

Is God pulling back the veil? Do you see this happening in your relationships with your family and friends? If you do, you are well on your way to freedom.

Let's take a look at how it affects our relationship with another very important person in our lives.

MY UNHOLY MEASURING STICK

Remember our litmus test that we used earlier to see if we carried PBT into our Christian lives? We asked if prayer and Bible reading made us closer to God. We saw that even after becoming a Christian by realizing that our efforts fall short, we often use our performance to gauge how close God is to us.

As I noted earlier, prayer and Bible reading are *very* important. They are *vital* to our Christian life. They are to be used to enjoy and experience the closeness we *already* have because of Jesus. Without them, we will never match our experience to the reality that God is indeed close to us. But those actions are not, and should not, be a measuring stick of how God is with us, loves us or is pleased with us.

But this is exactly what I did. The number of times I did my quiet times or devotionals was how I judged if God was with me or pleased with me. Instead of realizing that God is always with me and pleased with me because of Jesus' work on the cross, I made it about my actions. I exchanged God's work for my work. And that is not a good exchange. I got ripped off!

Instead of being secure in who I was (in Christ), I was constantly insecure (PBT road sign #2). Instead of enjoying God's intimate presence, I was busy trying to earn it. Why would I do that? Why would I try to earn something that God had already given freely as a gift (see Ephesians 2:8, 9)?

Didn't I know this truth? Yes, I did. I learned it in seminary. I taught it. I taught about how God is with us and pleased with us because of Jesus, not because of our own work and effort.

If I knew this and taught it, then why didn't it show up in my everyday life? Why was my experience so different? I see now that I did know it, but only in my head. It was only head knowledge.

I never applied this truth to my life. It was good theology, but it never made its way into practical everyday application. In reality, I didn't *really* know it. Biblical knowledge is always experiential, not just mental ascent. Knowing the truth as book knowledge is not really knowing it.

The reason it never made it from head knowledge to everyday life? Performance-based thinking. I had these boulders in my way. I had all this radioactive dust clouding my vision and thinking. Although I read that my performance fell well short of what God required for me to be with him (see Romans 3:23, 24), my PBT led me to other conclusions.

ROLLERCOASTER RIDE

Instead of feeling secure about my relationship with God. I constantly felt insecure, thinking I hadn't done enough. And when I felt distant, my solution was to work harder. I would try to read more. I disciplined myself to pray more.

I would go out and buy a new journal or a new Bible to spark my relationship with God. I would sign up for conferences and go to retreats to jump start my relationship with God again. I would try to serve God and others more.

Now, none of those things are bad. They are good things that God desires us to do. But they were never intended to determine my value as a Christian or how much God loved me.

You see, if I was completely secure in how God viewed me and how He was pleased with me because of Jesus (and not my actions), then those spiritual activities *would be very beneficial* to my relationship to God. But instead, I was trusting in my performance and how disciplined I was in order to maintain my relationship with God.

No wonder my Christian life felt like a rollercoaster ride. *My relationship with God was completely dependent on my performance.* It went up and down depending on how well I was able to keep up with all the things I was supposed to do.

This was tiring. I fought burnout. I cycled up and down. Can you relate to my experience? Have you felt the strain of trying to maintain something that only God can maintain? God started our relationship with Him and He is the one to maintain and complete it (see Philippians 1:6).

We will talk more about how to enjoy these spiritual activities in the right way later on. For now, let's focus on the real problem, our PBT. *Again, it's not our performance that's a problem, it's how we use our performance to determine who we are and our value that's the main issue.*

If you're starting to see how PBT affects your everyday life, your marriage, your relationship with your parents, your parenting, your job, your school, your interaction with friends, receiving from God, receiving from people, your walk with God, being a dog owner, being a good neighbor, your income taxes (ok, not really), then you are well on your way to freedom.

This is Phase A. This is the first and most important step on this journey to freedom. You must first recognize PBT in practical ways in your life, not just in theory. You've got to let God pull back the veil and see exactly how PBT affects us. We need to shine the light on this way of thinking. If it stays hidden, it'll never get addressed.

We need to illuminate our target so we can get our dynamite and blow it up! We need to obliterate the source of these problems and not just minimize the symptoms. We need to smash the boulders that are getting in the way of the kind of life, freedom and intimacy that God has intended for us. That leads us to Phase B.

But before we step into Phase B, let's take a moment to recap Phase A:

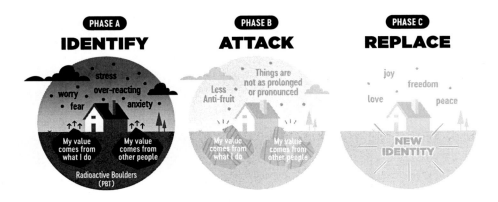

- Recognize anti-fruit in our lives (stress, worry, overreacting, etc.).

- Don't do symptom management and think that the anti-fruit is the main problem.

- Use the anti-fruit like guilt/obligation and insecurity/fear as road signs to identify your PBT.

- Start letting God show you ALL the ways PBT is practically showing up in your life.

Once you recognize the PBT in your life, you are ready to move to Phase B.

WHAT ABOUT MY LIFE?

1. When you've faced difficulties and conflict in your marriage or other relationships, what are things that you've done to address them? Have they created lasting change or are you still seeing the same patterns reoccurring?

2. Looking at these relationships again, can you see performance-based thinking influencing how you've been acting or responding to situations and people in your life? Describe ways you've seen PBT cause you to overreact.

3. Would you describe your relationship with God as a rollercoaster ride? How do you see PBT influencing your view of God and your relationship with Him?

CHAPTER 6

PHASE B: PLAN OF ATTACK

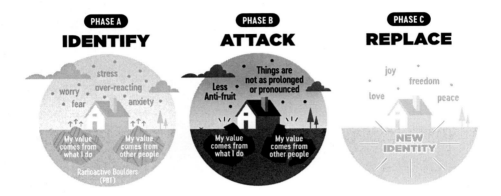

Through Phase A, we have learned to identify these radioactive boulders, which represent our performance-based thinking: deriving our value and identity from our performance and from others' view of us. These boulders are buried deep within us through years of influence from the world, society, parents, friends, coworkers, school, ourselves and even from the church.

During Phase B, we will focus on chipping away and removing the boulders that we've identified in Phase A. We will do this by attacking our PBT.

BREAKING THE BOULDERS

In this part of our process we will try to counteract this type of thinking. During Phase B, we will begin to experience more freedom once we loosen the grip that PBT has had in our lives.

When we start breaking the influence of PBT, the anti-fruit will start to lessen naturally. We'll see that when we correct our thinking and start experiencing life the way God designed, we will automatically have less anti-fruit.

As we begin to see how massive our boulders are, this task can seem very daunting. The good news is that we don't have to have this boulder completely destroyed in order to see substantial impact in our lives. We can begin seeing greater life and freedom right away. That's what is so amazing about this process.

FREEDOM PREVIEW

When we look at the landscape of our lives and how much PBT impacts us, we can get a preview of how much freedom and breakthrough is awaiting us. We can look at all these areas and see that they are ready to be transformed.

I've seen some people radically changed in a matter of weeks. With others I've seen the light bulb turn on after several months of addressing this. Whether it takes weeks or months, I'm always amazed by the miraculously quick transformation.

If you think about how long it took to build this pattern of thinking (20, 30, 40, 50+ years), changing the course of your life in a matter of weeks or months is nothing short of a miracle!

I've met people who've been in counseling for years to address issues in their lives without seeing significant change. But months after starting this process of breaking free from PBT, they've witnessed significant changes (often in the exact same areas for which they went to counseling).

In my own life, the change happened over the course of months. Each day God was revealing significant things to me. Every day God was showing more and more ways this thinking had invaded my life (Phase A) and then ways to chip a piece of the boulder off (Phase B).

I got a taste of more freedom and release daily. And when I did, it produced a hunger for more. It was a snowball effect. Each victory added fuel to the fire. I wanted more. It didn't matter that my boulders were so big, I saw it as an opportunity to experience more freedom.

I felt like God had me in a microwave (versus a crockpot). It was wonderful! I was breaking free from things that had had a hold on me for decades. I saw how this thinking wreaked havoc in many areas of my life but now was losing its grip. I was feeling freedom and life.

I began realizing that I AM NEW. I started seeing that what the Bible says *is really true for me*! Another wonderful byproduct of breaking this thinking was that the anti-fruit started to dissipate.

The process started with stress and anxiousness being less intense and lasting for shorter periods. Then it moved to having moments where it was completely gone! It's now gotten to the point where stress feels *abnormal*.

I still experience stress, but it immediately feels wrong. I have a new normal. I know what it's like to experience the kind of life Paul envisioned when he instructed us not to be anxious about anything (Philippians 4:6, 7).

I know it's possible to live that way. All the time? Maybe not, but much more regularly. It's something that I can pursue. Before, that would have been a dream world, not reality. I didn't even consider it or pursue it because it didn't seem possible.

This was just one anti-fruit. I wouldn't have enough pages to detail all the other anti-fruit that has been drastically reduced (worry, overreacting, guilt, fear, insecurity, anger, etc.). Remember, this is just a _side-benefit_ of breaking the boulders. This was a *great* side-benefit, but this was not even the main attraction.

The real show began when I started breaking free of the PBT boulders. After I made strides in breaking the boulders, I started seeing that there was nothing in front of me, hindering me. My path was clear.

I didn't have hoops to jump through. I didn't have dust in my eyes and things were clearer. I could see God. I could hear from Him more readily. I could be loved by Him unconditionally. I was unchained. I had no 150-lb. backpack. I was free!

Instead of being led by my own efforts and these boulders of performance and other people, I could now be led by God. It was not just something that I read about in the Bible. I was actually in a place to experience it.

I couldn't have had God leading before because I was too busy leading. I couldn't have the Holy Spirit take control because I needed to be in control. My performance and other people's views and expectations of me demanded that I stay in control.

Now, it's your turn. Are you tired of letting your performance and how others are judging you drive you? Are you sick of PBT turning your relationship with God into a roller coaster ride? Are you tired of waiting until you improve your performance or become more disciplined?

Are you ready to start feeling the freedom and life that is *supposed* to accompany the good news of the gospel? You need to be ready because you are going to have to rethink, and, in many cases, throw out things that you've believed to be true.

You have to be ready like I was when I began this journey. You have to conclude that the old way of living life doesn't work. You need to see that the old way is not God's design. It's not what the Bible prescribes.

INTRODUCING THE REPENTANCE TOOL

Our first plan of attack in Phase B is using what I call the "repentance tool". It's one tool that you may have already been utilizing. But we will see it's not the repentance that we might have grown up with in church. In fact, we might need to change how we view and experience repentance for it to be of any use in breaking our boulders. Let's look at a story about Good Friday to give us a backdrop.

IS GOOD FRIDAY GOOD?

When my daughter was young, I remember asking her about Good Friday. I asked her if she knew what Good Friday was and why we were celebrating this day. She said no, so I proceeded to explain that this was the day we remembered what Jesus did on the cross, dying for our sins. I told her that Jesus died on a Friday and then came back to life on the third day, Easter Sunday.

While I was explaining this to her, she had a troubled look on her face. I could tell something was bothering her. After I finished explaining about Good Friday, I asked her if there was something I said that concerned her.

She said, "Why do you call it *Good* Friday? This is not good! This is a bad day!" I knew exactly what she was talking about because I've had similar thoughts. I had that same question of why do they call Good Friday "*good*"?

Have you ever gone to a Good Friday service and left "feeling good"? I know I never have. I've never gone to a Good Friday service that felt joyous. It's odd that we say that we *celebrate* Good Friday. I've never been a part of a Good Friday service that felt celebratory. Easter Sunday? Sure. That is when the mood is celebratory, but never Good Friday.

I've been to countless Good Friday services where they depict all that Jesus suffered through on the cross. They talk about all the scorning and scourging He endured and all the pain He suffered. I've even seen churches bring out a person dressed in a robe wearing a crown made of thorns and carrying a cross to bring to life the things He endured on our account.

If you have been to similar Good Friday services, what are the predominant emotions and thoughts? Sadness? Mourning? Guilt? Disgust? Thinking you should be doing more? Thinking that you don't deserve this?

I think these emotions are all very common and I've experienced all of them. I've felt so unworthy thinking about Jesus on the cross. I have felt guilty, like I should be doing more for God. I should be doing more for all that Jesus had done and suffered for me. Have you had those same emotions and thoughts?

At this point, I want to take a step back and ask the question, "What is the reason why God sent Jesus to die on the cross?" What was God's motivation? What was His heart? Well, the Bible is clear on this.

> **John 3:16a:** For God so **loved** the world that he gave his one and only Son.
>
> **Romans 5:8:** But God **demonstrates his own love** for us in this: While we were still sinners, Christ died for us. (emphasis mine)

What does God want us to feel when we think about Jesus dying on the cross? Loved. Deeply loved. Incredibly loved. Unconditionally loved. Yet, is this how we feel when we think about the cross? Do we feel loved?

If you are like me, that's not the *first* thing that comes to mind when I think about Good Friday. But why isn't it? Why isn't our initial reaction feeling loved when we remember Jesus' death on the cross? If this is God's intention for us to feel loved by Jesus' sacrifice, then why isn't this the primary result?

Yeah, you guessed it. Similar to the prodigal son story we looked at earlier, PBT is the culprit. Because we base our worthiness upon our performance, we can't accept that the sinless Jesus Christ died for us. We can't accept this without it producing guilt and obligation (road sign #1). We don't measure up to this type of sacrificial love.

We can't make it even. What we have to offer seems like crumbs on the floor. We can't pay Him back. We feel guilty. We feel like we need to do more. *Even though we can't earn it, we feel like we should try to do more anyway.*

We feel *all* these things, but what we often don't feel is loved. We can't get past the boulders to let God's love come in. This is when a flag needs to rise up and an alarm needs to go off. We need to say, "Wait a minute!"

This is the gift God has given me in His Son, but I am not able to fully receive it. *He wants* me to feel loved but I don't feel loved. *I want* to feel loved, but I don't feel loved. Instead, I feel guilt and obligation.

What do we do? We recognize the guilt and obligation are coming from PBT. Then we use our sledgehammer to break the boulder. This is where we can pull out our Repentance Tool. Jesus dying on the cross is a great backdrop to this very effective tool we can use to break our boulders.

A BRAND NEW WAY

What is the first thing that comes to mind when you think about repentance? Fun and enjoyable? Incredible? This is something that I want to do every day, multiple times a day? Not even close?

This definitely would not have described my experience with repentance. Whether it was dealing with anger, impatience, lust or other persistent failures, I do not have good memories about confession and repentance. In fact, some of my lowest points in my Christian life were on my knees crying out to God concerning my sin.

Having repeatedly done the same things time and again, I would beat myself up. As a result, *repentance was something that I knew I had to do, but I never actively sought it out.* Then something changed.

What I want to present to you is the new perspective that changed my view of sin and repentance. It's a new way of thinking about repentance that not only changed my experience but chipped away at my PBT. It has become a tool that I use on a daily basis to break my performance-based thinking.

Let's start with the *old* way that I had developed in dealing with sin and repentance. This was typical of the experience I had for my entire Christian life. Look at the repentance diagram, which starts with a sin we need to confess and repent from.

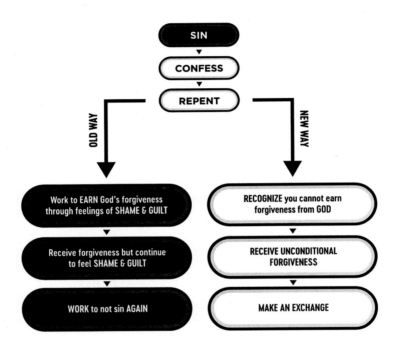

What would come next is that I would try to earn God's forgiveness. I would never say that was what I was doing, but, in essence, I was trying to earn his forgiveness through shame and guilt. I'd beat myself up about my sin. I tried to promise Him that I was not going to do it again. I would need to do these things **before** trying to receive forgiveness.

I couldn't *just receive* forgiveness after confessing and repenting. *I would, in a real sense, try to earn the right to be forgiven through demonstrating how bad I felt, by showing how guilty I was or promising that I was not going to do it again.* Whatever form it took, I would have to do something. I would have to offer something to make myself feel better about receiving God's forgiveness.

After I spent sufficient time earning forgiveness, I would feebly try to receive if I felt like I did a good enough job. Even after beating myself up, sometimes I still wouldn't allow myself to *feel* forgiven.

What is certain throughout this process, I definitely would not feel God's love and presence as a result of my repentance. Just like with the Good Friday example, I would not feel loved by God's forgiveness of my sin. I would not feel the love that prompted God to send his Son Jesus to die for my sins. Instead I would feel guilty, defeated and condemned.

What came next? I would leave that time and try my best not to sin again. *How* would I attempt to do that? It would be from my own determination and from my sense of shame and guilt. This was the driving force to help me in trying not sin again.

Dealing with sin by my own power and effort wasn't effective. Even with constant reminders that what I was doing wasn't right, my determination wasn't powerful enough to overcome the persistent sins in my life. That's when God brought a new way.

Now I say a "new" way, but it's not really new. It is actually over two thousand years old. It's the way that we find in the Bible. It starts out the same (look at the diagram again on p.66). We bring our sin before God. Next, you want to confess your sin and repent. You want to turn away from your sin. That's what God desires.

Here is where the paths diverge. After confessing your sin and expressing your repentance, you need to receive God's forgiveness. You need to see that you are undeserving, but *you must have no guilt and no condemnation*. This is where it gets a little bit touchy.

No guilt and no condemnation? No beating myself up about my sin? That doesn't sound or feel right. How can you repent without showing God that you really mean it?

Yet the Bible is clear on this topic. Romans 8:1 says, "Therefore, there is now *no condemnation* for those in Christ Jesus (emphasis mine)." There is also no ambiguity in seeing why Jesus came. He came to take away the guilt and the shame associated with our sin. He bore this on the cross (Hebrews 12:2).

But even with this knowledge, there is still a sense that it should not be this easy. If you don't allow yourself to feel any guilt, how could this possibly be right?

UPFRONT FORGIVENESS

I was teaching about repentance in our church, and there was a woman who stopped me when I got to this part about having no guilt and condemnation.

She raised her hand and said, "Can I ask you a question? I think that I follow you and this makes sense, but is it ok to feel *a little bit* of guilt?" I understood why she was asking because it doesn't feel right to feel absolutely no guilt when you are dealing with sin.

But there is a fundamental problem with trying to show God how bad you feel (or any other thing we feel like we need to do) in order to receive forgiveness. The problem is: *when* are your sins forgiven?

If you are a Christian and you accept Jesus' death on the cross, then that's when your sins are forgiven. *ALL* your sins are forgiven upfront—past, present, and future—all at the same time. *If all your sins were not taken care of, there is no way you could be in God's presence and have a relationship with Him.*

Now this is hard for us to take in because that is not how we experience forgiveness on a human level. If I were to do something bad to my wife and ask for forgiveness, then she could forgive me. But what if I committed the same sin against her repeatedly? After a while, she's going to stop listening to me when I say I'm sorry. She's going to have trouble believing and forgiving me.

I'm going to have to show her that I'm really sincere. I'm going to have to tell her what a jerk I am. I need to demonstrate to her how I really didn't mean to do that. I have to sincerely apologize because we don't forgive all of each other's sins upfront. It just doesn't happen like that.

When you get married and come down the aisle, the pastor doesn't say, "Do you take this man and do you take this woman to have and to hold and to *forgive every single sin they'll ever do in the future . . . right now?* Every hurtful word and act that they're ever going to do, I want you to forgive **right now**. If you agree, say 'I do.' (insert crickets. . .) Hmm. I said 'SAY I DO.' Hello?!?"

I have never seen it. But I think it's a great idea! Unfortunately, that is not how we forgive. The problem comes when we take our human experience and apply that to God. We think that this must be the way that He forgives too (needing the guilty party to show how sincere they are *before* He forgives).

Even though the Bible says He has already forgiven all my sins, we cannot accept that this is how it works. We need to go and show God how terrible we are, how awful we feel and then promise not to do it again in the future.

We need to jump through all those hoops before we allow ourselves to be forgiven. We do it because we need to jump through the same hoops when we repeatedly sin against people in our lives. But this is not true with God.

We need to see that a little bit of guilt is not necessary. Not only is it not necessary, it's harmful. *It's harmful because it puts us in a position where it is prohibitively difficult to receive the forgiveness and love that God has already given because of Jesus.*

Do you see the uselessness in trying to earn something that He's already given you? What do you think God is thinking when we come timidly to Him wondering *if* He is going to accept our apology for sinning?

What do you think God wants to tell us when we try to convince Him that it's ok to forgive us because we feel so guilty and ashamed? Do you think that He's swayed when we promise Him that we are not going to do it again? Or is He shaking His head?

If we are able to align our thinking to the truth that God has already forgiven all our sins upfront, we can then go on to just receive His forgiveness without trying to put conditions on it. Because if we put conditions on receiving His forgiveness, we'll never feel *un*conditionally loved and accepted by Him.

We can, and should, allow ourselves to recognize that we are undeserving because that is certainly the case. But in the next breath, we need to receive. Receive without adding anything else. Receive His forgiveness. Receive His cleansing. Receive His love and presence.

When we can receive knowing we aren't deserving, we will break that performance-based thinking. If we can receive without trying to earn forgiveness, we will sever the connection between our performance and His love for us. We will start experiencing Phase B, breaking our PBT boulder.

COMPLETE REPENTANCE

After we receive God's forgiveness, we still need to do one more step in our repentance. You see, repentance means "to change our mind and perspective" or "to turn around." In the case of repenting from our sin, that would mean turning away from our sin. *But turning away from our sin implies that we are also turning towards something or someone else.*

Did you catch that? We not only turn our back to sin, but at the same time we are turning our face towards something better. What are we turning towards? First and foremost, we are turning towards God. We are turning towards cleansing, forgiveness and love as we discussed above.

In addition to turning towards God, we are also turning towards the things that He wants us to do or the way He wants us to think (a new perspective). If we found ourselves yelling in anger, we need to ask God what He wants to give us in exchange for that. God could lead us towards love, compassion or patience.

That completes repentance. Turn away from anger. Turn towards God and love, compassion or patience (or whatever else God lays on our heart and mind). *Often, we are so focused on the sin, we lose the fact that we are getting something much better in exchange.*

Because of our performance-based thinking, our actions carry an inordinate amount of weight. As a result, our behavior becomes the sole focus of our repentance. *We never realize that the best part of repentance is not what we are turning away from but it's what we are turning towards.*

We can't be content with just being forgiven and cleansed from our sin. We need to see that God forgave our sin so that we can be with Him and be aligned with what He desires for us. If we can take our focus off the sin (which God already dealt with!), then we can receive what He wants to give us in exchange. This is the final aspect of the "new" way to approach repentance that we outlined on p. 66.

If we can take our eyes off our sin and failure, we can break the PBT tendencies. And when we break away from PBT and focus our attention away from our failure, we can then set our eyes on God and what He desires for us. This will give us a complete view of repentance. Out with the old and in with the new.

Are you starting to see the power of true repentance? The old, performance-based way of repenting that is focused on our work, instead of on God's work, doesn't produce this kind of exchange. It only produces anti-fruit. Let's start changing our minds about repentance.

We need to change our thinking about how to repent, what it is for and what it produces in our lives. If we can do this, our experience of repentance will completely be transformed. We will also be transformed, and we will break off more and more of our PBT (Phase B).

Are you ready to try? In the next chapter we will practice using the Repentance Tool. Before we do, let's recap what we've gone over.

We introduced the Repentance Tool as a way to combat our performance-based thinking boulders. But in order for this tool to be effective in battling against PBT, we must rethink and rework how we approach repentance.

WHAT'S OK:

- To confess and repent of our sin
- To recognize and feel undeserving of God's forgiveness

WHAT'S NOT OK:

- To try make ourselves feel better about receiving forgiveness by allowing ourselves to feel guilty, condemned and ashamed.

WHAT'S DIFFERENT:

- To receive God's upfront forgiveness without conditions

- To allow ourselves to acknowledge God's presence and love in the midst of our failure

- To see repentance as an exchange. To not focus on what we are turning away from but focus on what we are turning toward/gaining—God's presence and what He wants to give us in place of our sin.

WHAT ABOUT MY LIFE?

1. Describe what your experience with repentance has looked like in the past. Has it been a positive or negative time? Has it caused you to avoid times of repentance?

2. What ways have you tried to "earn" forgiveness and make yourself feel better about receiving God's forgiveness?

3. Identify persistent sins that you struggle with. This could be anger, impatience, lust, jealousy, being discontent, etc. Write those down here. These are the sins that we will need to address using the Repentance Tool.

_____

_____

_____

_____

_____

_____

_____

_____

_____

_____

_____

_____

CHAPTER 7

PRACTICAL APPLICATION
- REPENTANCE TOOL -

In the last chapter we introduced the Repentance Tool. We talked about a new way of thinking about and experiencing repentance. With this new approach, we can make strides in Phase B, eliminating PBT.

Now let's look at some real-life examples and practical steps we can take. Take note of each breakthrough as they used the Repentance Tool so we can learn how to practice on our own.

THE REPENTANCE TOOL STEPS:

1. Recognize, confess and repent of your sin and failures.
2. Receive God's forgiveness (without shame, guilt and condemnation).
3. Allow yourself to get a sense of Jesus' presence with you amidst your sin.
4. Ask Jesus what He'd like to give or show you in exchange for the sin you are turning away from.

GARY

Gary is not an alcoholic, but there are times when he goes out with his friends and he drinks too much. It's a pattern that he's seen happen in his life over the course of many years.

Every time Gary had too much to drink, he felt regret. He felt extremely guilty because he knew he shouldn't be getting drunk. He tells me that he's prayed and asked for forgiveness, but it still happens.

It's caused friction with his wife. She got very upset with him whenever he drank too much and then drove home. He was also upset with himself. He didn't want to continue this behavior.

I spoke to Gary about the things we discussed in the last chapter. I shared about how we *should* experience repentance and asked him if he was open to trying a new way. He agreed.

I instructed him to pray and ask God to bring to mind one instance of when he had too much to drink. Right away God brought a situation to mind. He and his friends were at a restaurant having a few drinks and he got carried away.

I asked him if he had confessed and repented of his sin of over-drinking at the restaurant that night. He said he had. Then I asked him if he could receive God's forgiveness without feeling guilt. He didn't feel comfortable with this, but I reminded him that God had already taken away the guilt and shame.

Next, I asked him to picture himself there at the restaurant with his friends. I had him envision Jesus there. He closed his eyes and tried to picture Jesus. He told me that he could (in his mind's eye) see Jesus there. He was sitting right next to Gary, in between himself and his friends.

I told Gary to pray and ask Jesus what He is thinking when He sees Gary drinking. Gary pauses and I remind him that it's ok. There's no guilt and condemnation. I said that Jesus was in fact there when all this happened and already knows the events of that night.

He proceeded to pray and ask Jesus what He thought. Gary got something right away. He felt like Jesus was saying, "You are believing a lie." He was surprised, and I was too.

We didn't expect to get that answer. It wasn't disappointment. It wasn't condemnation. It was God revealing the spiritual reality of what was happening. Gary had repented of his sin, and God was present and speaking to him.

I had Gary pray and ask what Jesus wanted him to do in response. Gary sensed Jesus was saying, "Focus on my presence." We spent some time doing that.

We thanked God for His presence with Gary during the past event. We thanked God for His presence with Gary right NOW while recounting his sin. We were both left with a sense of praise and thanksgiving.

Gary continued to share that he got a different picture of Jesus there with him and his friends. *He said that once he recognized Jesus' presence there, he didn't want to drink.* What he also noticed was that when he pictured Jesus there with him and his friends, they were still having a good time (even with Gary not drinking).

He recognized the lie that he was believing. The lie was that if he didn't drink with his friends that he wouldn't enjoy himself and his friends wouldn't either. Gary recognized this and repented of believing that lie. Wow! We praised God again!

Without guilt and condemnation, Gary was able to picture Jesus there with him in the midst of his sin. Having been forgiven, he was able to sense God with him. He was given insight that was beyond his own understanding. He realized that the lie he was believing kept him in this cycle.

Before, Gary tried to stop over-drinking, but it was through his own guilt and determination. Now that he was able to recognize God's presence, he was able to see that he wouldn't drink too much because he didn't *want* to. He was also able to hear from God about the lie he was caught in.

Do you see it? It was Gary's new nature being revealed. His new nature was to not drink too much. How did this happen? It was through receiving God's forgiveness without guilt and condemnation. It happened by letting go of his performance-based thinking and being in a position to receive God's presence and love.

By Gary letting go of his PBT, he left changed. He left full of hope and faith. A big chunk of Gary's boulder also broke off that day. He took a sledgehammer to his PBT boulder by seeing Jesus there with him *despite his sin*.

With his focus on God, instead of his failure, Gary got an exchange. He exchanged his old way of acting for his true nature. PBT was being broken (Phase B).

He was hesitant to try and envision Jesus there with him while he was drinking with his friends because of the guilt and shame. But when he moved past that, Gary experienced a real breakthrough. Pieces of the PBT boulder were demolished. Lies were exposed. Truth was revealed. Transformation happened.

LET'S REVIEW GARY'S STORY AND THE REPENTANCE TOOL STEPS:

1. He recognized, confessed and repented of his sin of over-drinking.

2. He received God's forgiveness (pushing past guilt and shame).

3. As a result, he allowed himself to get a mental picture of Jesus being present with him amidst his sin.

4. Because Jesus was present, God showed Him the lie that he was believing. He exchanged the lie with the truth (that he didn't need to drink to enjoy being with his friends).

WHAT ABOUT MY LIFE?

If you've struggled with a habit in your life, can you stop before moving on to the next example and go through the same steps as Gary? Practice going through the four steps and see what God shows you during this time of repentance. Go slow. Allow yourself to really be forgiven and cleansed.

Remember to continue until you've made an exchange. Turn away from your sin and turn towards God's presence, love and what He wants to give you to replace the pattern of behavior or thinking.

Write down in the space below or in a journal what you are hearing from God during this time.

_____

_____

_____

_____

_____

_____

_____

_____

_____

_____

_____

_____

_____

_____

_____

_____

_____

_____

_____

_____

_____

RICHARD AND EVERY MAN'S BATTLE

Richard is a godly man I've known for many years. He loves God with all his heart. But Richard has been carrying guilt for a long time. He's been carrying a heavy weight and it's been a *huge* hindrance in his relationship with God. He struggles with watching pornography.

Richard is racked with guilt and shame. When he struggles, he wants to hide. He doesn't want to go to church. He doesn't want to go to Bible study. He doesn't want to pray. He doesn't even want to go to work.

He's tried over and over to stop his behavior. He's beaten himself to a pulp when he falls into temptation. He's promised God that he would stop, only to fall again.

I shared with him that this a common struggle that many Christian men have (I've heard countless stories like his). I shared with him that it's easy to feel like he's the only one struggling, but that's a lie. This kind of sin causes us to isolate ourselves from God and other people.

Guilt and shame have debilitated him. The heavy burden of carrying this shame has sapped any and all energy that he has. This self-condemnation is keeping him from God.

I told him that he should not be feeling guilt and condemnation. He had a perplexed look on his face, like he couldn't believe what I was saying to him. I said it again, "You can't let yourself feel guilt and shame."

I could tell he was still confused because he was speechless. After a while, he blurted out, "How can I do what you're asking? How can I *NOT* feel guilty and ashamed when I'm doing something *so* shameful?!?" **I told Richard that what he was doing *is* shameful. However, Jesus took the shame of what he was doing unto Himself.**

I asked him if he was willing to let Jesus do that for him. I asked him if he was willing to let Jesus take the shame that is associated with what he was doing. I encouraged him to let go of that shame and allow Jesus to take it.

A waterfall of tears began streaming down his face. He couldn't speak. He was sobbing. After a little while he nodded his head. I had him go to Jesus and ask for forgiveness. He asked for forgiveness for carrying guilt and shame when Jesus had died to take it.

I asked Richard to open up his hands and offer Jesus his shame and guilt. Through his tears, he gave it all to Jesus. *All the years of debilitating guilt and shame were given to God.*

Then we continued to the next step. Richard had already been forgiven, but he needed to receive God's love and acceptance. I communicated to him the next step would be difficult. But if he wanted to be free, this would help him on his journey.

I had him picture a time when he fell into temptation with pornography. Then I asked him to envision Jesus there with him. I could tell right away he was *extremely* uncomfortable with what I was asking. I reminded him that Jesus died to take the shame. I implored him to not let what he did keep Jesus away.

Richard pictured a time in his study when he fell into temptation, and then he tried to imagine Jesus there with him. All of sudden he started weeping again. After a few minutes, I checked in with him and asked if he could share what he was envisioning.

He tried to compose himself. He told me that it was very hard picturing Jesus there with him, but he tried to continue. When he did, he was shocked by what he saw. He envisioned Jesus in back of him, holding him from behind.

He pictured Jesus holding him tight. Richard could sense that Jesus wanted to let him know that he was loved. He couldn't believe that Jesus was holding and loving him at the time when he was doing something so awful.

Richard was overwhelmed with emotion. He knew that Jesus didn't approve of what he was watching, but Richard was too overwhelmed by God's love for him to make that the focus.

After our prayer time was over, we were left thanking and praising God. Richard felt like a gigantic weight had been lifted off his shoulders. He felt a freedom that he hadn't felt in a long time.

We debriefed together about what happened. I asked him if he ever thought it was possible that he'd be able to experience something like what he had just experienced. "Never!" was his response.

He said if I wasn't there challenging him with the truth about his guilt and shame (and PBT), there was no way he would have allowed himself to give up his shame or to allow himself to envision Jesus there with him. We both thanked God again for an incredible, miraculous time of repentance.

LET'S REVIEW RICHARD'S STORY AND THE REPENTANCE TOOL STEPS:

1. He confessed and repented of his sin **and** of not letting go of his guilt and shame.

2. He received God's forgiveness (and gave God the shame he was carrying).

3. This empowered him to envision Jesus there with him, holding him.

4. He exchanged the shame and condemnation for God's incredible, unconditional love for him. He exchanged bondage for freedom and release.

Did you hear that? It was a giant piece of boulder crashing to the ground. Pushing past the PBT cracked Richard's boulder. That's what opened up the possibility for God to come and move in such a powerful way. He took away the guilt and shame that Richard had been carrying for years.

This couldn't have happened before. Because of PBT, Richard couldn't break free to let God take his guilt and shame. *His actions and failure were too big. As a result, he never felt forgiven nor had a sense of God's presence and love for him.*

When God broke through, Richard recognized that he didn't have to carry guilt and shame any longer, because Jesus took that upon Himself. Do you see how Richard went against his PBT by allowing Jesus to take his guilt and shame even though he didn't deserve it?

Richard broke the stronghold this thinking had in his life when he let God love him in the midst of his sin. The result was freedom and intimacy with God that he had never experienced before.

Guilt, depression, shame and hopelessness were replaced and exchanged by God for life, freedom, hope, love and faith. All this came through a time of repentance! This was possible because Richard intentionally went against his old, PBT tendencies.

Since this time, Richard is free. He rarely struggles with pornography and when he does, he is able to receive God's forgiveness and not be overcome with guilt and shame. This is the fruit of Phase B and experiencing true repentance.

God broke the hold of pornography that had a grip on Richard. Through using the Repentance Tool and counteracting PBT, Richard has gotten his life back. He is experiencing more of the life and joy that God intended.

Can you see how powerful this tool can be? The power comes from what Jesus did for us on the cross. But we can't experience it if we feel the need to carry the guilt, condemnation, and shame all over again. When we break free from our PBT (Phase B), we will allow ourselves to receive the life and freedom that God gave us through His Son.

WHAT ABOUT MY LIFE?

If you struggle with pornography, lust or other things that produce shame and guilt in your life, I want to encourage you to reread Richard's story and put yourself in his place. As you do, ask God for the courage and grace to be forgiven and not condemned. Pray and ask God to be present with you and give you something in place of the shame and condemnation.

Go through the same four repentance steps that Richard went through. Be open to God revealing Himself to you and showing you His love and acceptance because of what Jesus has done.

Record what you are receiving from God here or in your journal:

_____

_____

_____

_____

_____

_____

_____

_____

_____

_____

_____

_____

_____

HELL HATH NO FURY

Francis has been a Christian for almost her entire life. She accepted Christ at a very young age. She's married and has three wonderful kids. But like Richard, Francis has been carrying a heavy weight.

Francis has been struggling with her anger. She doesn't know where it comes from. She grew up in a Christian home. She has a good marriage. Her kids are well-adjusted and have a good relationship with God. Yet there are times when she has uncontrollable anger.

When her anger spikes, she lashes out at her husband and her kids. She feels a tremendous amount of guilt. When she thinks about her precious children, she is overcome with guilt and regret. She knows what she is doing is wrong. She knows that her kids don't deserve to be yelled at and berated.

She tells me that she would pray and ask God to take the anger away. But every time she prays, all she can think about is how awful she feels about her outbursts. She says she asks God to show her where the anger is coming from. But whenever she prays, she can't hear anything from Him.

I asked Francis if she'd be willing to do an exercise with me. She agreed and I took her through the same exercise using the Repentance Tool that I took Gary and Richard through. I had her pray and ask God to bring to mind one of the incidents where her anger flared up. She joked with me that there were too many to choose from.

However, she had one particular memory that came to mind about her yelling at her kids. She told me that she had already confessed and repented of her anger during this incident. Then I asked if she could receive God's forgiveness without guilt or shame. She said that it would be difficult but she would try.

I had her picture herself getting upset and yelling at her kids. Then I asked her to envision Jesus there with them. I reassured her that it was ok to do this. Jesus was indeed with her during this time and He was also there with her kids. She agreed.

She started to picture the moment. She said that when she tried to envision Jesus, He was there. But what disturbed her was that Jesus was standing over her kids. He had his arms covering and shielding them.

She said it looked as if Jesus was trying to protect her kids from a predator. She thought that He was protecting them *from her*. She was horrified by the image.

She had an overwhelming sense of guilt and shame. I tried to assure her that she was forgiven. Then I had her pray and ask Jesus what He was thinking during this time. What He said surprised her. He didn't condemn her.

What He said was, "I've got them. They are mine. I love them. You don't have to control them. These are my kids. You don't have to try and micromanage them. You don't have to keep pointing out everything that they are doing wrong.

You don't have hold on so tight. You don't have to worry so much. I've got them. These are my kids. I love them. You don't have to criticize them so much. You can let go of fear. See me and release the fear."

While she was relaying this to me, her whole demeanor changed. Through her tears, she went on to tell me that she sensed something literally had changed inside. She felt like she could finally let go. She felt free. She didn't feel condemned by God. Instead, she felt loved by Him.

God loved her kids so much that she could let go of control. Francis felt a release. She saw that her anger was coming from her need to control her children. She was so concerned about the mistakes they were making. She wanted to protect them, but what she was doing was actually hurting them.

She was trying to control their life and future. And when she felt out of control, she couldn't handle it. When her children weren't cooperating, she lost it. The result was the anger and lashing out.

When Francis was able to see God in the midst of her anger, things became clearer. She saw that God loved her kids more than she did. She saw that God was covering over them, protecting them. She saw that He had them in His arms. She didn't have to hold them so tightly.

She realized that when she was holding them so tightly, God couldn't come in. She needed to let God love them like He was loving her right now in all her brokenness. She had to let go and let God love them and take care of them.

She felt transformed. She felt free. She felt relief. She felt relieved of the weight and responsibility she was carrying for her kids and their future. Francis was able to give that responsibility over to God.

She was full of praise and worship. She finally heard from God! And when she did, He took the burden. He replaced her guilt with freedom. He replaced her shame with love—His love for her (even in the middle of her blowing up at her kids) and for her children.

I pointed out that she probably never heard from God before because she was too focused on her behavior and hadn't allowed God to come in. She agreed with my assessment. She said that she was consumed with her guilt and couldn't see God *even if He was there.*

LET'S RECAP FRANCIS' STORY AND THE REPENTANCE TOOL STEPS:

1. She confessed and repented of her anger and treatment of her children.
2. She received forgiveness from God despite the feelings of guilt.
3. She was able to sense God's presence there with her and her children in the middle of her failure and hear Him speak to her!
4. She exchanged control and anger with release, trust and love.

God's presence changed everything for Francis. It revealed the truth that she could be with God and hear from Him even though she had this persistent sin in her life. This ran counter to her PBT. *Receiving in the midst of sin breaks the hold of PBT (Phase B).*

God showed her that she couldn't have seen this truth before because her performance-based thinking made her focus solely upon herself and her failure. Once the PBT was broken using the Repentance Tool, she was free. Free to be loved and free to let God love her kids.

Do you see a pattern developing? When you release guilt and shame, you give God freedom to come in. Since God has already taken the guilt and shame, we unnecessarily put up a barrier that prevents Him from coming in to love and restore us. We need to let go of guilt and shame and break our PBT tendencies.

WHAT ABOUT MY LIFE?

Are you ready to try this new way? Are you ready to abandon the old way of dealing with sin and repentance and receive what God sent His son Jesus to give?

If you are ready, you need to start putting this into practice. Our experience and our PBT are not going to change on their own. They are not going to change by simply reading this book. Even if we recognize the truths in this book but never put them into practice, change will never take root in our lives. We'll never experience the freedom God wants for us.

Here are the steps that you can use to practice right now:

1. **Ask God to help you recognize a sin in your life He wants you to confess and repent from.** If you are like me there could be many, but ask God to highlight one (we can save the others to do more practice). As you read the stories above, God may already be speaking to you about a certain sin. If so, use this time to address that sin.

2. **Try to picture the event again.** As we saw in the stories above, the next step is to revisit a time when this sin occurred. Where were you when this happened? Who was there? What was going on? What were the events surrounding your sin? Don't be afraid to feel all the emotions you felt during that time. God is there. It's safe. **Then receive His forgiveness and let him take any guilt and shame.**

3. **Try to get a mental picture of Jesus there with you during this time.** If you have trouble, just acknowledge that *He is and was present* during this event. If you feel your sin was especially shameful, this could be difficult to do. But you must go back to the truth. God was actually there with you and He is not ashamed of you.

4. **With God there with you, ask Jesus what He thinks about you, your situation and your sin. Then ask what He wants to show you or give in** *exchange* **for your sin (this is an important step).**

Finally, when you are done, it's time to worship. Give God the praise and thanksgiving He deserves. Let him know how grateful you are for what He's done.

Take a moment to sit before God and go through these steps. Please don't rush through the steps like you are doing the dishes. Go slowly and let God lead your time.

Use this space to write down in your journal, or below, what God speaks to you while using the Repentance Tool.

RECAP USING THE REPENTANCE TOOL

How was that experience? Did it put you in a better position to receive His forgiveness and sense His presence and love for you? Did God show you what to exchange for the sin or lie you were believing during this time?

When I first started to adjust my thinking and experience with repentance, I had difficulty sensing God's presence. As we discussed, it was because I could not allow myself to entertain the idea that God might be present with me after I sinned (PBT).

If that's the case with you, you need to take a step of faith. When we cannot sense God's presence with us (the fruit of the Spirit is a good indicator of God's presence—it's found in Galatians 5:22, 23), we must make a declaration. Even when the feelings aren't there, we must declare and thank God that He is indeed present and loves us. This will help break PBT.

We cannot let our feelings dictate truth. Feelings need to follow truth, not the other way around. If we demonstrate faith based on the truth that Jesus already has forgiven us, the feelings will eventually follow suit. God honors our faith and will help us get a sense of His presence.

This is not positive thinking. This is based on truth. During the early stages of breaking PBT, I had to keep reminding myself of the truth, even though my feelings didn't match. My feelings were attached to a lie. It took time to realign my feelings with the truth. Exercises like this one helped to do that.

Please keep in mind that this takes time. We need to walk through these steps repeatedly. Whether this was a positive experience or not, we need to keep being intentional to break free. We must continue doing this regularly. Don't be afraid to keep addressing your sin.

Don't allow the performance boulder to bring false fear. It's not true that you get your value from what you do. You are not defined by your failures. *Don't be afraid of asking God <u>daily</u> to show you sin that has crept up in your life.* Then use the repentance tool to experience more life and freedom and to break your PBT.

We do this in order to **RECEIVE**. We don't do this to beat ourselves up anymore. We do this to enter into God's presence. We don't do this to be racked with guilt and shame.

Final note on repentance: We might need to ask God to bring healing from our past experiences with repentance. If so, we'll need to repent from how we've been repenting.

We might need to receive forgiveness for trusting in our own work instead of Christ's finished work on the cross. This could be necessary before starting to use the Repentance Tool on a daily basis. However, we *do* need to make this a daily part of our lives to break PBT.

If we want to be free, we need to implement this into our life. You will see results. You will see results because what Jesus did for us has power. His sacrifice has the power to transform and set us free.

[If you need additional help in this area, there is more on repentance in the bonus material at the end of the book.]

In the next chapter, we will look at one more tool to help us on our journey to freedom.

CHAPTER 8

THE REFLECTION TOOL

In this chapter I'm going to introduce you to another tool that you can use during Phase B of our journey to freedom. This is a simple but powerful tool that you can use on a regular basis to combat PBT. You can use this tool to break apart your radioactive, performance-based thinking boulders.

In order to introduce this tool, I want to revisit our Journey to Freedom Diagram.

Notice the three phases that we mapped out earlier:

Phase A: **Identify** PBT using anti-fruit
Phase B: **Attack** the PBT boulders
Phase C: **Replace** performance-based identity with our new identity

The tool that I want to introduce implements the first two phases (A and B) and gives a preview of the third phase (C). It is called the Reflection Tool and it builds off of what we have learned up to this point. Let's go over the simple process and then look at several examples. As we go along, I'll give different tips on how to apply this tool in our lives.

It is called the "Reflection" Tool because this is a time where we will ask God to bring up incidents that He wants us to address and reflect back on. We will look back on what we were thinking and feeling and then ask God to reflect back the truth about these incidents.

Here are the basic steps:

THE REFLECTION TOOL STEPS

1. **Recognize anti-fruit in your life.** As we learned in Phase A, anti-fruit acts as a signal for PBT in our lives. Ask God to show you any anti-fruit that is evident in your life. Just like we did with the Repentance Tool, we need to revisit the scene.

   Picture the time when you experienced the anti-fruit, then try to envision Jesus with you. (Note: As with the Repentance Tool, if you have trouble visualizing Jesus, just try to get a sense that He's with you despite your actions and direct your attention to Him)

2. **Identify how the PBT boulders are impacting your actions, thoughts or reactions.** With Jesus there with you, ask Him if you are getting your value from your performance and/or from what others are thinking about you. I've noticed that many times it's coming from both. (Note: After a while, you can skip step one and go directly to this step when God reveals one of the boulders in your life.)

3. **Denounce the lie.** It's a lie that performance or other people determine your value and identity. You want to expose and then denounce the lie. This is best done out loud.

   You need to simply but assuredly say to God (and yourself), "My value doesn't come from (this result or this person). Those things or people *do not have that power over my life, only God determines my value.*"

   This step is really the meat of Phase B, where we attack the boulder directly and counteract our performance-based thinking.

4. **Replace it with the truth.** Now that you have denounced the lie about who are you and where you get your value, replace it with the truth about how God truly sees you. With Jesus there, ask Him how He sees you. If you are having trouble hearing from God, just thank Him that you are an unconditionally loved son or daughter.

   [*Note: Step 4 of the Reflection Tool provides a preview of Phase C on this journey to freedom.*]

Let's start taking out this tool and swinging away at the boulders. We will do this by targeting the PBT boulder and how getting our value from others affects us. In each case, we will take a look at real-life examples of how this boulder shows up. We will examine the impact PBT has on our perspective and our choices.

PBT PUTS US ON THE DEFENSIVE.

When we place inappropriate weight on what people say or think about us and our performance, it puts us on the defensive. *It shows up when our reactions to criticism are over the top.* When we are defensive, the emotional fireworks inside of us are not proportionate to what's happening on the surface.

THREE-RING CIRCUS, PART III

I didn't forget! Remember how I said that you needed to wait to see exactly how God transformed my marriage? The wait is now over. Here it is . . .

It was a three-ring circus in our home as little arguments turned into huge battles. It would start with small things like, "How come you didn't put the cap back on the toothpaste?" or "How come you squeeze the tube from the middle instead of from the end?"

It started small and ended with us bringing up other, totally unrelated issues and comparing our laundry list of things we had done or said. It concluded with saying things that we would come to sorely regret.

We were no longer arguing about toothpaste or the trash. We were arguing about something that was happening inside of us. There was no winning this kind of argument. There was no amount of proof that we could bring to the table to win the argument because it wasn't rational anymore. We were arguing about the emotional fireworks inside, not about the circumstances.

There was a cornucopia of rotten anti-fruit that came from these arguments. Anger. Frustration. Guilt. Insecurity. Fear. Hopelessness. Condemnation. Needless to say, the first part of using the Reflection Tool was not an issue. It was easy for me to recognize the anti-fruit (**Step 1**).

The part of Step 1 that didn't come as easily was to picture myself arguing with my wife and then trying to envision Jesus there. Like we went over in the previous chapter, I needed to get past the guilt and shame. When I did, I would move to **Step 2**.

What was the source of all this anti-fruit? The change came, not when I tried to manage or avoid the symptoms, but when God showed that it was stemming from my PBT boulders. God showed me that I was getting too much of my value from what my wife thought about me. When I saw the real problem, I was ready to address it.

It was the fact that I was standing on a shaky foundation that caused these emotional eruptions. It was because I was getting my value from my wife instead of from God that my reactions were so over the top. This was the real problem.

Here, I would move to **Step 3**. I would acknowledge Jesus was there and *I would declare, "My value doesn't come from what my wife thinks about me. My value doesn't come from what she says about me. God has not given her this authority over my life."*

That's it. There weren't ten steps to follow. It was denouncing the lie that my value and identity came from my wife. This broke the power. It was not a trick to fool my mind or positive thinking. It was based upon the truth.

The truth is I don't derive my value from her or any other person. Only God has the power and authority to determine who I am. That's why breaking this boulder's hold on me was as simple as recognizing the lie and shining the light on it.

In **Step 4**, I replaced the lie with the truth. I asked God how He saw me. I declared that I'm an unconditionally loved son. I declared that I'm secure not because of what my wife said but because of what God says about me. I'm beloved. I'm a friend of God. I'm a child of the King.

It seems so simple, but it was SO POWERFUL. Through the Holy Spirit's illumination, I was able to identify the lie. The words that carried so much unbearable weight began to dissipate. I started to experience what Jesus declared in John 8:32, "Then you will know the truth, and the truth will set you free!"

I felt free. I felt release. I felt the heavy weight lighten. It went from fifty tons to fifty pounds. It still felt heavy in the beginning, but it wasn't crushing. Before, I had to go into survival mode and become ultra-defensive. I would strike back and turn the spotlight onto my wife. Now, I didn't need to do that.

Did I still have frustration, fear, insecurity and the other anti-fruit? Sure. But the *intensity and duration* dramatically decreased. This is the initial progression into Phase B and breaking PBT.

Previously, when we had arguments, it would handicap me the entire day and sometimes even longer. When I started to use this Reflection Tool, I began seeing that the after-effects of her words would only last minutes instead of hours.

I also started to see that the intensity of those emotions diminished. Before, I would need to find an escape because I couldn't deal with all the anti-fruit. Now I didn't feel the need to do that. My boulder was cracking.

As I continued to do this, more change occurred. Through the regular reflection time with God, my thinking started to change. I started seeing things more clearly. I started to genuinely believe the truth that my value didn't come from my wife. What happened next?

I started to do Step 3 of the reflection process, not *after* we had arguments but *before!* When she would say something that caused my defenses to spark, I would denounce the lie. When I could feel something bubbling inside, I would make the declaration, "My value doesn't come from what she says about me. My value *only* comes from God."

In the past, my reaction to something negative she said about me would have been a ten out of ten. Then it started to subside: five, three, one, and sometimes, zero. Not all the time, but sometimes nothing! I would have no negative reaction! I didn't feel or act defensively.

As I mentioned before, I'm not saying that what my wife says about me is not important. I'm not saying it doesn't carry weight, but it doesn't determine who I am. She doesn't have that power over my life. God never intended that. Only God determines my value and my identity. No other person can do that, not even my spouse.

The tide was turning. The helpless feelings were being replaced with faith and hope. The discouragement and depression were being exchanged with life and freedom. I experienced freedom from anger, freedom from the need to be defensive, and freedom to address the issues God wanted to change in our marriage.

I was being transformed. I was being made new. *Really, I wasn't being made new. I was starting to experience the true identity I already had in Christ.* As my boulder and wrong thinking started to subside and the radioactive dust cleared, I began to see what was there all along. I began to see that God *did* make a change. I really was a new creation. But now I put myself in a position to experience it.

As I exchanged the lie for the truth about who I am (Step 4), I genuinely started to believe that I'm valuable because of how God sees me. He sees me as His own. He sees me as His child. He loves me unconditionally because of Jesus and not because I'm a good husband.

This is a very important step. We can be satisfied just by doing Phase B (breaking PBT). I was ecstatic with the changes that were happening by denouncing the lies and breaking the boulders. I could have been very content with the anti-fruit subsiding. But I started to see that was just the beginning.

If I didn't replace the lie with the truth, I would be doing this denouncing forever! No, I needed to fill this void with the truth. By leaving my old faulty source of identity, I could now replace that with a new solid foundation.

Now, every time I exposed the lies, I would then affirm the truth. I affirmed the truth of who I am in Christ. I started stepping into my new identity in Christ. I would ask God what He thought about me and how He saw me.

TEARING DOWN THE TENTS

When I started to experience this breakthrough, I shared my excitement with my wife. To my surprise, she was skeptical. But when I thought about it, it really shouldn't have been so surprising.

This change happened very rapidly. It took place within a matter of months. Most of the change was happening inside of me, where only I could notice.

How could I expect that after years of knowing me and having to deal with my insecurity and defensiveness, she would suddenly believe that I had undergone this miraculous change? I knew she wanted to believe. But the part of her that bore the scars and hurt made her hesitant to fully embrace that I had changed.

In the past, her reluctance to believe that I had genuinely changed would have hurt me and made me defensive. I would have felt the need to prove to her that I had indeed changed. I would have felt prompted to detail all the ways that I had been behaving and responding differently. But my response was different now.

I didn't feel defensive. This boulder was losing its hold on me! I didn't get my value from what she thought. I didn't need her to recognize this change for me to really believe and embrace it for myself.

I knew that God had shifted the tide. I knew that if He kept the momentum of what He was doing, that eventually my wife would see it. I knew the *tents were about to come down and the three-ring circus was going to pack up and leave...*

And I was right.

Initially, my wife didn't acknowledge to me that I had changed. We had friends over at our house. The guys were in one room watching sports. The ladies were in the next room. My wife was talking to one of the women when I heard my name. It got my attention.

What I heard next caught me off guard. I overheard my wife telling her friend about how I had changed. I heard her saying that we had been arguing so much less and that I had undergone this dramatic change. Wow! I knew that I had changed but when my wife acknowledged it, it was an enormous validation of what God had done.

You know you have been significantly transformed when your spouse, who knows you better than anyone else, says you've changed. You know God has done something dramatic when the person who has seen the best *and worst* of you says that you're different.

Now, I didn't *need* her affirmation. I knew already that I was drastically different, but it sure was nice to hear! It was the icing on the cake.

I could now address present issues without dealing with the past pain. I started being able to see the objective truth about what my wife was saying. I could not have done that before.

Whether it was true or not, I couldn't receive it either way. I would be too defensive. I couldn't hear what she was saying. My defensive wall would block it out. I couldn't hear her heart.

But now I could hear what she had to say even if it was something negative about me. I could objectively ask the question of whether it was true or not. If it was true, I wanted to hear that from her. I wanted her to help me step into who I am as a husband and a father. I wanted to move towards who God made me to be.

If it was not true, I wasn't going to receive it. I would tell her that I didn't believe what she was saying was true, but the volume and intensity would be completely different from before. I would say it gently and calmly. Sometimes, I wouldn't even need to communicate it at all. That marked a significant shift from how I responded in the past.

The transformation that occurred in me was nothing short of a miracle. All this came from repeatedly using this simple but powerful Reflection Tool. The dramatic change stemmed from addressing my PBT boulder. This enormous shift took shape by denouncing the lie and replacing it with God's truth. But is it really that simple? Is it that easy?

Yes! It is that simple because that pattern of thinking doesn't have power over the life of a believer. God has restored his original intent for our lives when we receive Jesus. We no longer need that faulty foundation. Without God, PBT was what we had to resort to. That is no longer the case.

Other people don't have that kind of power over us unless we empower them. They don't have that authority unless we give it to them. They don't have that level of influence unless we allow it. By recognizing and denouncing the lie, we pull the plug.

We disallow that lie to have a place. It's that easy because it doesn't really have power. When we recognize the truth, it disables our old PBT. It's like when you go into a dark room and turn on a light. The darkness *automatically* leaves. It's that easy because God's truth has the power to dispel darkness.

Step one – recognize the anti-fruit. Step two - have God reveal if you are getting your value from the PBT boulders (performance and others). Step three - denounce the lie. Step four - exchange the lie for the truth of who you truly are. Yes, it is that easy. You can break free.

PBT MAKES US CRITICAL

When we derive our value from what we do and others' view of us it makes us critical. If we think that our value comes from people assessing us and our performance, then it's only natural that we're going to do the same thing.

If other people are judging us and basing their judgments on what we do or what we look like, it's understandable when we in turn judge other people using the same standard. When we take our seat in the judge's chair, we become very critical of others and their mistakes.

SANDY

Sandy is a mid-level manager at a manufacturing company. She is in charge of several people but she also has supervisors managing her work. Sandy tells me that she constantly feels judged by people.

She says that she gets it from all sides. The people she supervises judge her based upon how good of a manager she is. At the same time, her supervisors are also judging her and how well she manages. She feels a tremendous amount of pressure at work.

Sandy has physical problems. She has headaches. She has back problems. She has trouble sleeping at night. She is overweight because she is constantly eating. She is eating to stay up later. Eating because she is stressed. Sandy is not happy.

When we discuss this boulder, she is overcome with the truth. She knows that this performance boulder is alive and kicking in her life. She knows that it is not only present, it is HUGE.

Sandy talked to me one day after church. She shared how she felt like she was under a microscope. Not only did she feel like people at work were watching her every move, she also felt this from her parents.

Her parents were constantly telling her about things that they didn't like about her and what she was doing or not doing. They think that she should have chosen a better career and question her about why she's not married yet.

Because of this scrutiny, she had also become very critical and judgmental. She didn't want to be. She knew that God didn't want her to be, but she said that she couldn't help it. She found herself gossiping about other people. She talked behind people's backs, tearing them down.

She was critical of people at work. She saw people as lazy or dumb. She was critical of her supervisors. She talked badly about them to other mid-level managers. She was bitter. She was not happy about her attitude, and she recognized that this came from her PBT.

I asked Sandy if she wanted to break free from this. She immediately said yes. I proceeded to take her through the Reflection Steps. I started by having her pray and ask God to highlight some anti-fruit that had been prominent lately. Right away she had a list of anti-fruit. We began with her judgmental attitude.

I had her picture a time when she was being judgmental. It didn't take long for her to come up with a situation at work where she felt like she was judgmental. She said that she was having lunch with her coworkers and she was saying negative things about her supervisor. I asked her to picture herself in the restaurant with her coworkers, then envision Jesus with her (Step 1).

She told me that she could picture Jesus there. She started crying. She conveyed how she didn't think that she'd see Jesus, but He was there! I asked her to keep praying and ask Jesus what He thought about her judgmental remarks.

What God did next was unexpected. Sandy shared how God pointed out that she was getting her value from other people (Step 2). But for some reason, He was bringing her mom to mind, not her boss or coworkers. Sandy felt like God wanted her to address the relationship with her mom.

She prayed and ask God if she was getting her value from what her mom thought of her. She started to cry again as she nodded yes. I had her move to Step 3. She needed to make a declaration. I asked her if she knew that it was a lie that she got her value from her mom. She said yes.

I told her to denounce this lie that she had been believing. She went on to repent first. She told God that she was sorry for believing this lie. She was sorry that she had given her mom this power that God never intended. I could see on her face that her heart and mind were changing.

She prayed and told God that it was a lie that her value came from her mom. She repeated again that her value didn't come from what her mom said about her. She went on to say how only God determines her value.

We both sensed God's presence and the wonderful work He was doing. After a few moments of soaking this in, we went to the last step. I had her now affirm the truth. I had her ask Jesus how He saw her.

Very quickly, she blurted out, "Loved! He says that I am loved! He says that He is my Father and that He loves me. He says that He doesn't love me because of what I do. He loves me because I'm His."

We both praised God. We both thanked Him. We thanked Him for his goodness and love. We thanked Him for exposing the lie, pointing out the real source of the lie, and then demonstrating His love for Sandy.

THE AFTERGLOW

A couple weeks later, I got an email from Sandy. She shared a story about how she was at work and some of her coworkers were gossiping about one of the people at her company. Instead of joining in, she shared about how this woman they were talking about was going through a hard time with her family. The gossip stopped.

She then asked them if it was ok if they said a quick prayer for their coworker. They agreed! They prayed for this coworker that they were bashing a few moments before. God authored a transformation.

Sandy had been transformed. She was experiencing life and freedom. This breakthrough she shared in the email didn't happen through her own determination to stop gossiping. It happened naturally. She didn't want to gossip! Then God spoke to her.

God led her to think about what was going on in this other coworker's life. Sandy prayed with the same coworkers that she used to gossip with. She made an exchange. She exchanged judgment for compassion and love. She changed the atmosphere at her workplace.

Anti-fruit (judgmental attitude) revealed the PBT boulders. These are Steps 1 and 2. God came in. He highlighted her mom. He shined the light in the dark place to dispel the lie (Step 3). The truth set her free. God met her. She exchanged the lie for the truth of God's unconditional love for her (Step 4).

Once God gave her the target, she was able to blast her boulder! The result? Transformation. *What she couldn't do through her own effort and trying, God did for her*. It came naturally as a result of changing her thinking and letting her true, loving nature come out.

WHAT ABOUT MY LIFE?

Carve out at least ten minutes. Go slow. Don't race through these steps. Allow yourself to engage God. This is not just an exercise. This is time to interact with Jesus. This is the time to pray and have God's hand come in to break the hold of things that don't rightfully have a place in your life.

Before you begin, here a few *helpful tips*:

1. **Don't read the questions and simply think about the answer. We need to ask God first.** After we ask Him, we can continue with what He brings to mind. We need to engage Him. That's why I have people try and picture Jesus. It's a way to focus on Him and how He is guiding our thinking.

   As we saw in the previous examples, surprising things happen each time questions were directed to Jesus. So before delving into the answers on your own apart from Him, acknowledge God's presence here with you. Let Him direct your thinking.

2. **The after-effects.** Sometimes when you are thinking about a time when anti-fruit popped up, you may be unable to make a connection to the PBT boulders (Step 2).

   For example: There was a time when I got frustrated helping my kids with their homework. There was anti-fruit (impatience, frustration and stress), but did it come from getting my value from helping my kids or what they thought about me? I didn't think so.

   I took a step back and looked at what happened earlier that day, it was clear that I was getting my value from other people. *The frustration I felt helping my kids was the <u>after-effect</u> of the stress and anxiety I was feeling earlier.* The stress from earlier that day *was* connected to my boulders.

When you can't make a connection to the PBT boulders, pull the camera back to get a wider shot. Pan back to see what had been happening earlier that day or that week. Maybe it is a different event that God wants you to address to break your PBT.

3. **Don't worry if this process doesn't come easily.** It takes practice. Take note that in previous examples I was with each person guiding them. Even if you are able to just recognize the anti-fruit, that is a win.

    Recognizing the anti-fruit is an important step on the journey. As we talked about with symptom management, it's easy to let the anti-fruit go unnoticed. Recognizing the anti-fruit and declaring this is not the normal Christian life is a big shift in the right direction.

4. **Don't worry if your change is not as *dramatic* as the previous examples.** There are many other examples where the change is more subtle. *I've had more small wins than large ones.* And the tally is not even close. But the changes are still significant. It's the small gains that produced the long-term change in thinking.

Here are the steps that you can use to practice right now:

1. Pray and thank God that He is present with you before you begin. Then **ask God to bring to mind any anti-fruit** that you've been experiencing (stress, anxiety, condemnation, insecurity, anger, overreacting, etc.) when interacting with people. Whether at work, at school, at home, in the car or at the coffee shop see what God brings to mind. **Go ahead and picture the event that brought the anti-fruit.**

2. Once you get a mental picture of that event, envision Jesus there with you (remember even if you feel ashamed, He already took the guilt and shame, so let Him come in). Ask Jesus what He thinks about the situation. **Ask Him if you are receiving your value from others or performance, or both.**

3. With God present, **make the declaration that getting your value from others (or performance or both) is a lie.** It is best if you declare this out loud. Say, "I don't get my value from this person (or result). This person (or result) doesn't have that power over my life. Only God determines my value."

4. Now try to picture the scene again with Jesus there with you. **Ask Jesus how He sees you (as opposed to how you see yourself or how others see you).** Ask Him what He thinks about you. If you are not sensing anything from God, just affirm that you are indeed his unconditionally loved child. Then thank Him that you are His son or daughter. Thank Him that He loves you unconditionally.

Close your time praising Him for what He's done.

Use this space, or a journal, to write down what God speaks to you while using the Reflection Tool.

_____

_____

_____

_____

_____

_____

_____

_____

_____

_____

_____

_____

_____

CHAPTER 9

PRACTICAL APPLICATION
- THE REFLECTION TOOL, PART II -

From the previous chapter we saw how receiving our value from other people's opinions can severely impact our relationships. Our PBT can cause us to be defensive and critical when we feel insecure and judged by others.

In this chapter we will examine two other effects that PBT can have in our lives. After reading real-life examples, we will continue to practice using the Reflection Tool.

PBT LEADS US TO BE UNFORGIVING

This is a big one. Our PBT boulders can cause us to be more unforgiving. If we're deriving our value from what other people say, their words become *overinflated*. This can lead us to hardening our hearts towards those who have hurt us.

When people say things that are critical of you, it's going to hurt. And if these people are close to you, especially family, we are going to experience profound hurt. When this criticism occurs repeatedly, the wounds get bigger and deeper.

When we believe our value comes from what people say, these words carry more power and weight. They are like daggers that pierce us inside. When this happens over the course of years, you can imagine the scarring that occurs. Sometimes this wounding gets so severe that we reach a tipping point.

An event will happen that pushes us over the top. Someone criticizes us one too many times and we lose it. We can't believe how horrible this person is and how they are treating us. We might blurt out that we hate them and never want to see them again. We harden our hearts. We've tried to forgive in the past, but now we're done. We can't forgive them anymore.

I've seen this time and again. I have seen families broken apart by unforgiveness. They cannot forgive because it hurts too much. It hurts so much that they can't let it go. They can't release the hurt and forgive. They are in a prison of unforgiveness. It impacts their ability to see and receive from God and other people.

How does it get to this point? Unforgiveness happens slowly over time. It's *accelerated* by our performance-based thinking. It happens because we allow people like our parents, siblings or spouses to determine our value. And when we allow this thinking to fester, their words carry more weight than God ever intended.

Our value is not supposed to come from what our family and friends think about us or what they say. But if we allow ourselves to think this way, then those words are going to cut deep. This is especially true if the hurt is coming from someone who is supposed to love and care for us. Instead of care and love, we're getting hurtful words hurled at us.

I do want to point out that even if you have the right thinking and your identity in place, these words are still going to hurt. We're still human. But the difference is if we correct our thinking, these words aren't going to bring us to the place where we cannot forgive. When we take the air out of their words, we'll see that it will impact us, but to a lesser degree.

THE GREAT WALL OF CHINA

Bobby is a man in his mid-forties, but he says his father treats him like he's twelve. He shares how his dad has always been hard on him. His father has never been affirming to him. He has never told Bobby that he loves him. On the contrary, he has always been critical of him. He shares how his father doesn't think Bobby can do anything right.

His father's favorite phrase is, "That's stupid." Whenever Bobby tells him about anything that he is thinking or doing, his father says, "That's stupid." That's the kind of feedback Bobby gets. He says that eventually he just had to put up a wall.

His father's critical words just became too much. As a means of survival, Bobby had to put up a defense. Nothing his father said was going to affect him anymore. He made up his mind that whatever his father said, he was just not going to receive it.

It was self-preservation. He didn't want to totally cut himself off from his father, but this was the only way to handle it. From that point on, whenever Bobby saw his father, he would put up his shield. Bobby would hear his father's criticism, but he wouldn't comment on it. He wouldn't receive what his father was saying. He just put up his defenses.

There was a problem. Even though he erected a wall, it wasn't impenetrable. Hurtful words still went into his heart. It still hurt whether Bobby admitted it or not. Worse yet, it really affected his relationship with his dad. His heart was hardening. Unforgiveness was settling in.

Bobby knew there was a problem, but he didn't feel safe enough to address it. He didn't think that he could forgive and let everything go. I took Bobby through the Reflection Tool. The anti-fruit was abundant. Anger. Stress. Unforgiveness. Frustration. Overreaction. This was Step 1.

I had Bobby pray and ask God to bring to mind one time when his father criticized him. It didn't take long for him to recall something. It was a family gathering. They were celebrating Bobby's youngest daughter's first birthday. In Bobby's culture, a child's first birthday was a huge affair. They rented a banquet hall and invited over sixty immediate family members, extended family, and friends.

At this event, Bobby's father was very vocal about how he didn't think the room was set up correctly. He told Bobby that he needed to change the arrangement. His father told him that he should have been better prepared and that this was typical of him.

Bobby was fuming. In front of his family, he yelled at his father and told him to be quiet. He told his father that he was ruining the party. Bobby blurted out that if his father loved his granddaughter he'd stop complaining.

His father was not happy. He was silent throughout the whole party. He didn't talk to a single person. He left without speaking to Bobby. Bobby felt terrible. He was torn. He felt angry with his father and, at the same time, felt guilty that he yelled at him in front of family.

I asked Bobby if he had already addressed the sin on his part. He said he did confess his anger to God when it happened. God had forgiven him, but there were still things that needed to be addressed.

I asked him to picture this scene again. Then I had him envision Jesus there with him and his father. He was initially hesitant, but he tried.

After a long while, he said that he was able to picture Jesus there. He was having trouble with what he saw. He said that he was confused because he envisioned Jesus holding his father. He asked aloud why Jesus was not holding him. He was the one that really needed God. Bobby asked me if I thought God was angry with him.

I told him that God had already dealt with his sin. He had already forgiven him. I asked him to engage God again. He went on to pray and ask God why He was holding his father.

After a while, Bobby responded. He said he believed he was getting his value too much from what his father thought about him and what the others at the party were thinking about him (Step 2). He continued to share how God was showing him something else.

God started bringing to mind Bobby's grandfather (his father's father). He explained that his father's father was a very successful businessman. He was a well-known and respected person in their community.

He was also very hard on Bobby's father. Bobby remembered how his grandfather would belittle his father all the time. He recalled how nothing that his father did was good enough for his grandfather.

As God was revealing this to him, tears started coming down his cheek (Bobby is NOT emotional at all). He came to the realization that not only was he getting his value from his father, but his father was getting his value from his own father (Bobby's grandfather). He saw his father's pain. He saw his father's hurt. He saw how crippled his father was. More tears. He realized why Jesus was holding him.

Bobby spent time repenting. He repented for his unforgiveness. He repented for all the harsh words he had spoken to his father. He repented for the wall that he had put up. He repented from getting his value from his father. He declared that this was a lie (Step 3). He prayed and asked God to make an exchange (Step 4).

Bobby asked God how He saw him, but also how God saw Bobby's father. God said "You are *both* my sons." He said He loved each one, but He loved them together. He made them to be together, not separate. Bobby knew what God wanted him to do.

The problem with putting up a wall as a defense mechanism is that it goes both ways. Not only does it stop anything from coming in, but it also doesn't allow anything to go out. In order for something to go out, one would need to drop the wall.

On that day, God blessed Bobby with a renewed sense of love and compassion for his father. But he knew that he couldn't express it because of the wall he had erected between himself and his father. He had a greater appreciation and love for his father yet knew he couldn't communicate this until he dropped his defenses.

Bobby couldn't drop the wall in the past because it would have left himself too vulnerable. But once he started to see that his father was not responsible for his value, it gave him the freedom and courage to drop the wall.

He made a conscious choice to be vulnerable and engage his father. Even though this meant he would allow the negative things to come in, he wanted to drop his defenses so that he could express his love for his father. I encouraged him to go through the Reflection Steps when he interacted with his father with his wall down.

He shared with me later, that even though their relationship was far from where he'd like it be, it was a new beginning. He felt like they were able to engage a little bit more. He had been able to show his father how much he cared about him, and his father actually received it!

Bobby got a two-for-one deal. Following the Reflection Steps, he was able to see the lie that he had been believing but also saw that this was true for his father as well.

As a result, Bobby experienced freedom. He was released from the prison of unforgiveness. He was free to forgive. He was free to love. He was free to be a son—to both his earthly and heavenly father! When his PBT boulder was addressed, it enabled Bobby to experience this newfound freedom.

WHAT ABOUT MY LIFE?

Can you relate to Bobby? Do you have people that are close to you that have hurt you deeply? Instead of protecting and caring for you, they have consistently said things that have come against you.

It is understandable and normal to feel hurt by these words and these people in our lives. What God doesn't want is for those words to carry more weight and power than they should. These people cannot determine our value or who we are.

To counteract this and receive healing like Bobby did, we need to let God come into our painful past and bring a new perspective. Before moving onto the final story using the Reflection Tool, take a few moments to ask God to bring to mind a person whom you've had a difficult time forgiving.

Follow the Reflection Steps by asking God to bring up a particular incident where they had hurt you with their words and/or actions. Then go through steps 1-4.

Remember, forgiveness doesn't mean you have to trust them again. It also doesn't mean that you give them permission to hurt you again. What it does mean, is that you release this person to God and release yourself from the prison of unforgiveness.

You are doing this to be free. Using the Reflection Tool will help reduce the weightiness of their words and help restore peace into your heart.

Here is a recap of the steps:

1. Ask God to remind you of an incident involving this person. **Acknowledge the anti-fruit** you were feeling or thinking.

2. With God present there with you, ask Him to **show you ways you might have been deriving your value from what they said about you or your performance.**

3. **Denounce the lie** by declaring out loud that your value does NOT come from this person or your performance. (Note: if it is especially painful, you might have to declare this multiple times.)

4. Ask God how He sees you and **declare the truth** about your true identity. If you have trouble hearing from God, declare that you are a beloved son or daughter of God who is loved unconditionally.

Take some time to record what God shows you and speaks to you below or in your own journal:

_____

_____

_____

_____

_____

_____

_____

_____

_____

_____

_____

_____

_____

_____

_____

_____

_____

_____

_____

_____

_____

_____

PBT TURNS US INTO PEOPLE PLEASERS

It makes sense doesn't it? If we believe our value comes from what others think, then it will naturally lead us to become people pleasers. If we increasingly get our value from what other people think, we will desperately want them to like us. Our desire for them to think well of us will drive us to do everything in our power to please them. Can you relate to this?

The problem is when we try to be people pleasers, we can never please everyone. Not only is this ineffective, but it causes you to focus more on what other people are wanting instead of what God wants.

You start to prioritize other people's expectations above things you should be devoting your time towards. *You make assumptions about what other people expect of you even when it's not communicated.* This is what drives you, instead of God driving you. Instead of God dictating what you do, this boulder is in the driver's seat.

EVERYBODY LOVES AMANDA REVISITED

Remember Amanda? Homecoming queen. Popular. Insecure. Depressed. Her mom was desperate to get her help. She was hurting so much that she couldn't leave the house to go to school. Nothing was helping. She finally agreed to meet with me.

As we met together, it was not difficult to recognize the anti-fruit. She was dealing with severe insecurity, fear and anxiousness. I had her pray and ask God to bring to mind an instance when she felt insecure (Step 1). Surprisingly, she chose the night that she was crowned homecoming queen.

I asked her to describe her feelings. She said that when she was standing in front of the crowd, she felt like a fraud. She shared that she didn't deserve to be up there in front of everyone. She felt utterly insecure with everyone looking at her. I explained about the PBT boulders and then I asked her to envision Jesus there with her.

She said that she couldn't do that. She declared that there was no way Jesus was going to be there. I asked her to consider that Jesus might be there for other people who were there that night (I tried the backdoor). She tentatively agreed.

Suddenly, I saw that God was doing something within Amanda. I could see it on her face. I didn't know what He was doing, but I saw her whole countenance change. Amanda was smiling (her mom said that this was the first time she had seen her smile in months).

I checked in with Amanda. I asked her if she could tell me what she was envisioning. She told us that Jesus was there on stage with her. She said that Jesus was telling her not to be concerned with what other people were thinking (Step 2).

He told her that she was up there *for Him*. He thought that she was a princess. He said that He was the King and that would naturally make her a princess. He said that this had nothing to do with how attractive she was, but it had everything to do with who He was. He was the King and He chose her to be His daughter.

Since Jesus already took her through Step 3 (denouncing the lie of what others think) and Step 4 (affirm her true identity), I prayed and asked that God would keep bringing these truths to mind. We joined together in praising God, the homecoming King! Amanda left beaming.

The following week Amanda emailed me. She told me that she was back at school. She thanked me for helping her break out of the deep pit that she was in. She confessed that going into the reflection exercise she had zero hope that it would do anything. She told me that she was so glad that she was wrong!

I was glad too! I was more hopeful going through the process than Amanda. I was more hopeful because I've witnessed countless people set free by recognizing lies and focusing on God's truth.

Amanda didn't change who she was to be set free. It took a change in her thinking. God had already made her His daughter, a princess. She had to realize that her worth wasn't tied to how attractive she was or others' opinions about her. It was true because of what God thought of her.

*Note: In dealing with cases of depression, **not all depression stems from performance-based thinking**. But I do believe that PBT is a major contributing factor that often makes things worse. In some instances, seeking counseling and the care of a psychiatrist is helpful and necessary. However, even in those severe cases, addressing PBT will be important and will help bring long term solutions to the insecurity that often leads to depression.*

RECAP

People pleasing is an easy trap to fall into. On the surface there's nothing wrong. We are trying to help people, care for and love them. But when we allow people in our lives to determine how we think and feel about ourselves, we have allowed them into a place that God never intended them to have.

There's a problem when we can't say no. The problem is that when you try to please everyone, you end up pleasing no one. Once you try to accommodate one person, you start letting another person down. You will feel the pressure and strain trying to please everyone. You will be left with nothing for yourself, for God or for your family.

Another problem is that you may spend all your time trying to be what others expect of you. You'll never know who you truly are and how God designed you. The good news is you can start reversing this trend. You can use the Reflection Tool whenever you face these situations to start breaking the lie that people determine your value. You can break free from the hold of PBT.

WHAT ABOUT MY LIFE?

Take some time right now and ask God to bring to mind a person that you find yourself trying to accommodate and please. Ask God to remind you of a specific situation where you did this and how it created anti-fruit in your life (stress, burn out, anxiousness, fear, etc.). Then go through the four steps like Amanda did.

Here are the reflection steps again:

1. Ask God to remind you of an incident involving this person. **Acknowledge the anti-fruit** you were feeling and thinking.

2. With God present there with you, ask Him to **show you ways you might have been deriving your value from what they said about you or your performance** .

3. **Denounce the lie** by declaring out loud that your value does NOT come from this person or your performance. You can declare this multiple times in order for it to settle into your heart.

4. Ask God how He sees you and **declare the truth** about your true identity. If you have trouble hearing from God, simply declare that you are a beloved son or daughter of God who is unconditionally loved.

Take some time to record what God shows you and speaks to you:

_____

_____

_____

_____

_____

_____

_____

_____

_____

_____

_____

_____

_____

_____

_____

MOVING ON FROM PHASE A AND B

The two tools of Repentance and Reflection are to be used regularly. Practice these daily. Take time in the morning. Review the steps for a few minutes at work during lunch or after the day is over. You need to develop this into a new pattern to break the old pattern of thinking.

Use the Reflection Tool when you sense anti-fruit appearing. Use this tool in situations that *often* bring anti-fruit (like Bobby seeing his father, taking a test, speaking in front of others, hearing criticism, etc.).

You need to practice so that you can experience the freedom that people in this book have experienced. Think about how long you've held onto your old way of thinking. You need to put time and commitment into breaking the patterns.

Before moving ahead to the third and final phase, spend time practicing these two tools. After you've experienced some momentum and freedom, continue reading to see what lies ahead.

In the next chapters we will venture into the third and final phase of our journey. Up to this point, we've covered a lot of ground on our journey to freedom.

LET'S REVIEW:

- After practicing Phase A and using the anti-fruit to identify where PBT is active in our lives, we can move to Phase B.

- Phase B involves directly attacking our PBT. There are two tools that we introduced to help break apart our PBT boulders: the Repentance Tool and Reflection Tool.

- The Repentance Tool is effective in trying to receive from God (His forgiveness, love and presence) even though we've failed and carry guilt and shame. When we can receive in the midst of our failures, we will break PBT.

- The Reflection Tool is a great way to not only identify when we have PBT surface in our lives, but also to defuse the power it has had over us. We also are able to exchange these lies we've been believing about ourselves with the truth about how God sees us.

LIVING **FREE**

KEEP IT GOING!

After traveling a long way on our journey towards freedom, we want to stop and enjoy just how far God has taken us. God has opened our eyes to how we've allowed the performance-based thinking virus into our lives and how rampant its effects are.

The scales have been removed so that we can see the reality of what has been a significant underlying issue in our lives. We can't underestimate just how HUGE this revelation is!

We've witnessed account after account of people being set free from these boulders blocking their paths. Hopefully, you have also been able to do the same. If so, the freedom and release you've experienced is just the beginning.

Let's take a moment to thank God for what He's done.

ARE WE THERE YET?

After we have seen the light, it's very important that we try to keep up the momentum that God has started. One way we can do this is by continuing to use the Repentance Tool and Reflection Tool every day.

We don't want temporary relief from PBT, we want a permanent separation. After having those two boulders drive us for all our lives, we can be free.

Keep seeking, knocking and asking God to bring up sin or anti-fruit in your life. You don't need to be afraid to do this because your value no longer comes from your actions. Allow God to continue redeeming these negatives by using them as a springboard to set you free.

As you break apart the boulders of performance and what others think, you will put yourself into position to move on to the next phase on our journey to freedom in Christ.

THE THIRD AND FINAL PHASE

Now that the dust has cleared, we want to take a look further down the road at Phase C. In this final phase, we will examine our post-PBT life.

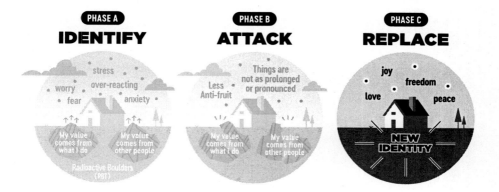

In Phase C, *we will <u>replace</u>:*

- **Our old PBT life for a new post-PBT life.** We will look at examples of what this new life can look like.

- **Our old thinking with new thinking about our performance.** This is very important. If we don't have a new way of thinking we will default back to our old PBT.

- **Our old performance-based identity with our new identity in Christ.** Up to this point, we have spent the entire book chronicling our *mistaken* identity. Now we will look at the other side of the coin at our *true* identity.

Finally, we will look at the finish line. We will get a glimpse at what ultimate freedom looks like. We will see that it may not be what we had imagined. And we will also see that this is not the end but just the beginning. Phase C will set us on the right course for the rest of our lives.

In the next chapter, we will start looking at the first two aspects of Phase C: our post-PBT life and our new way of looking at performance.

CHAPTER 10

PHASE C: REPLACING THE OLD

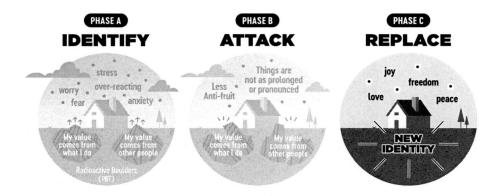

After going through Phase A and B of our journey to freedom, we are now ready to step onto new ground. In Phase C we will begin replacing the wreckage of our PBT life with the life that God created us for. During this new season, we will need to learn how to walk in our new life and new found freedom.

REPLACING OUR OLD PBT LIFE

Do you remember my story "No Free Lunches"? It was a story about celebrating my grandmother's birthday and how I learned that I can't receive from people without reciprocating. That's why it's difficult to let someone treat you, be ok bringing nothing to a potluck, or receiving a Christmas gift without having given anything in return.

Now look at my post-PBT experience:
I was out to lunch with a friend. When the bill came, we did the same song and dance about how were going to handle the check. Was someone going to pay or were we going to a pay for the check separately? That day, my friend wanted to treat me.

Normally, my first reaction would be to fight him as I had done in the past. I would tell him that he didn't need to do that. Even if he did treat me, I would have to add on that I'd pay for him next time.

But something changed on that day. I didn't fight him for the check nor did I say anything about it being unnecessary. Instead, I told him how much I appreciated him and his friendship and how blessed I was that he was treating me to lunch.

I was no longer under the influence of my performance-based thinking that required me to make things even or caused problems receiving. What also changed was everyone's experience of our time together.

Instead of neither person feeling blessed by one of us paying, both of us left feeling blessed. I felt blessed by my friend treating me. He felt blessed by giving since I didn't ruin it by making it feel like an obligation to pay him back. I was free to express my heart of gratitude and thanksgiving. He was able to express his heart and care for me.

I was thinking about that day and it brought joy to my heart. I was joyful because I was free. I was able to receive from someone and allow myself to be loved and cared for. My heart was feeling full because I let my friend pour into me. This is a picture of my post-PBT life. Free to be loved.

I would have never been able to experience any of that before. I would have been too focused on myself. My friend got to experience exactly what he wanted. He got to know that I felt blessed and appreciated. Now, isn't this the way God would have intended us to experience our time together?

I shared this same story "No Free Lunches" in a class called Freedom 101 where I taught about breaking free from PBT. Here's an email I received from one of the participants in the class:

> *Hi Sam!*
>
> *During your class this past Sunday, you talked about receiving without having to give in return. I am the worst receiver you can possibly meet, but God has been working on me since last Sunday.*
>
> *On Sunday, my family went to our friend's house and they treated us to yogurt. They also wanted to treat us to boat rentals at the lake, but I INSISTED on paying (of course, to even things out a bit).*

Yesterday, as I was talking to my cousin about going to a day spa this weekend with another friend. I shared how I couldn't justify getting a massage (expensive), but that I was just going to get a pedicure (the cheapest thing there.)

She said that she had some gift cards to the spa and that she wanted to just give me one. All I would have to do is take her out to lunch. I said that I couldn't do that. But as I reflected on this overnight, I graciously accepted her offer today. Not easy, but I did it.

Also, today I had a friend give me a really nice letter and a whole bunch of fruit, veggies and green tea to say "thank you" for my friendship. That too I accepted graciously, and I shared with her how God has a sense of humor and how He has been working with me.

It is cool how God has been working on an area in my life that is very difficult. Everyone always tells me that I am a bad receiver. Hopefully, I will be better as God is showering me with opportunities.

Blessings, Rachel

Do you see the freedom that Rachel is starting to experience? She is actually letting others care for her. And when they do, she is able to receive it without the sense of obligation to give back! These are small examples of things that happen daily where we can experience greater life and freedom. This is a small snapshot of our post-PBT life.

TIME AFTER TIME

It was a Monday morning and my wife and I were trying to get the kids ready for school. At the time, I was the one who dropped off both kids at school. As usual, we were running late. In the past, this would have made me very anxious.

You see, I hate being late. My dad raised me to think that if you are not five minutes early, you were late! Even though my friends were late all the time, I always had to be on time.

So on mornings like this one, I would have been stressed out. I would have started pushing both my kids' to hurry up. I would *strongly* encourage them to hurry and get dressed. I would firmly, and not so gently, exhort them to go brush their teeth and eat breakfast. When they would not listen, I would raise my voice louder and louder.

Although it would be effective in getting them to move faster, *everyone* would now be stressed out. I would be anxious, my kids would be anxious and my wife would be upset with me for yelling at the kids.

This morning was different. I was very calm. I had realized that I had been getting anxious about being late because I cared too much about what people thought about me. I denounced the lie and replaced it with the truth that we would try to be on time because I liked it, not because I got my value as a parent from others' view of me.

Interestingly, the kids must have thought I was *really* angry because I was saying everything *so softly and calmly.* They got ready faster than I had ever seen them get ready. I have to confess that I didn't tell them what was really going on!

There was more peace that day and my home was filled with more calm than storm. And ever since, I've experienced more peace in getting ready to go places. I'm no longer stressed when I'm running late. When I feel the stress creep up, I just remind myself that my value doesn't come from being on time or what others think.

Since I made this shift, you might wonder if I'm late more often. The answer is no. I'm still on time the majority of the time. But my experience is TOTALLY different.

I don't feel nearly as anxious now. I'm on time because this is how God made me. I'm still on time for the most part (just like before) but now it's not because I'm so worried about what others will think of me if I'm late. It's simply because this is who I am naturally. Also, if I'm not on time, it doesn't affect me like it did before.

The key: I still have the same routine, but my EXPERIENCE of it is completely different. As a result, I'm in a better position to hear from God and not stress out my wife or kids. I can enjoy getting somewhere without being anxious, and I'm able to think about other people versus being focused on myself.

Did you catch that? I'm still doing the same things as before, only my experience and perspective have totally changed. Instead of anxiety, stress and worry, I have peace and joy doing exactly what I did before. This is post-PBT life.

WILL I LOSE MY JOB?

After another one of my Freedom 101 classes, a gentleman came up to me to ask a question. He said that he was beginning to understand that PBT was a bad thing, but he was concerned. He was an executive in his company and his question to me was, "If I don't get my value from what I do, will I ever be able to get anything done?"

I understood his concern, I had similar types of questions. If we no longer obtained our value from our performance or what others thought, would we be as productive as before? The stakes are higher, but this situation is similar to the story about trying to be on time.

Even though we let go of our PBT, it doesn't mean that we can't be as successful or effective as before. In fact, sometimes we can be even more productive.

As I shared in the 150-lb. backpack analogy, when we are not carrying the burden of others' expectations, people pleasing and getting our value from what we do, we can actually do more, not less.

When we are able to receive freely from others and from God, we can accomplish more as a result. When we are loved unconditionally and our hearts and spirits are full, we have the energy and freedom to accomplish more.

Without PBT, we can hear from God about what we are doing without the clamor of other people's voices driving us. As a result, we can do things differently and more effectively. Our post-PBT life can be more abundant than ever before.

PREEMPTIVE STRIKE

A good friend of mine named Clyde took one of my Freedom 101 courses. After attending the course, he shared with me these stories in the months that followed:

Clyde was a business consultant. He had consulted for Fortune 100 companies and reported to upper-level managers and executives. He shared with me about a couple of different incidents that occurred while he was consulting on projects.

In one instance, Clyde was getting ready to report a key update on a major project to his onsite supervisor. Typically, Clyde would try to think of every possible scenario and would go over things with a fine-tooth comb. He was always super prepared for everything he did and he would spend several angst-filled days getting ready for these types of presentations.

But this time, trying not to earn his value from what his supervisor thought about him and his performance, he found himself not preparing nearly as much as he normally would have. He was a little unnerved going into the meeting, but he wanted to trust more in who God made him to be than in his own performance.

He was surprised when the supervisor told him after the presentation just how well he did. His report was glowing. Clyde was glowing. He began to realize that who God made him to be was enough to do the job. He started to realize the *extra* work he did was a result of getting his value from his performance and fear of what others were thinking. He saw that it wasn't as necessary as he had believed in the past.

The second situation was during another consulting project, where he was presenting to a room full of executives. Normally Clyde would feel a lot of anxiety before and during the meeting. Knowing this, he made a "preemptive strike." *Instead of waiting until after he felt worried and anxious, he did the Reflection Steps BEFORE the meeting (that's a great strategy!).*

He went on to explain that he entered the meeting very calmly. The presentation he gave was one of the best he had ever given. He felt God's presence the entire time. He commented on how this was the most natural and authentic he's felt in giving a presentation of that magnitude.

That is a picture of true freedom and the post-PBT life that God intends for us. We need to realize that when we shed our PBT, we can be more of who God made us to be. We will realize that who we are in Christ is more than enough to tackle any circumstance we face in life.

So, can you accomplish as much if you don't let your value and identity come from performance and what others think? You bet you can. Not only can you accomplish as much as before, you can potentially do more!

Not only is it possible to do more, you can be even *more effective* than you were before. Not only can you accomplish more and be more effective, your experience in doing the work will be filled with calm and peace. I might even go as far as to say you would actually enjoy it!

POST-PBT LIFE RECAP

What can we learn from the stories that I just shared about our post-PBT life? First, we can experience new life and freedom in everyday events. Whether it's going out with friends, getting ready to go somewhere, or doing a project at work, we can live more freely than ever before.

The second thing we can learn is we will be doing many of the same things as we did before, even while ridding our lives of PBT. The big difference is that our experience will be so much better! Instead of anxiety, stress and worry, we will have peace, joy and love. *We will start seeing that who God made us to be is more than enough for what He's called us to do.*

Now that we have a glimpse of the kind of life that we can experience in Phase C, let's turn our attention to what will help us experience more of this freedom for the long haul. To make this change lasting, we need to adopt a new way of thinking.

How *would* God have us view our performance? *If we never develop a new way of thinking, we will naturally default back to our old way of thinking. Not because we want to, but because we don't have another alternative.* As we continue into our post-PBT life, we need to focus on how God views our actions.

WHAT ABOUT ALL THE COMMANDS IN THE BIBLE?

As we travel into Phase C, we will need to brace ourselves. After spending our time denouncing the power that performance has over our lives, we now have to re-engage performance again. Even though we don't get our value from what we do, we still must accomplish things in life.

There's no better place to start examining this than in the Bible, because it speaks a lot about performance. There are literally hundreds and hundreds of commands found in the pages of God's word. It's easy to feel like the Christian life is all about performance and obeying these commands.

We'll begin by looking at God's original intent for the commands He has given to His people. To do this, let's look at the very first commands He gave to Adam and Eve. In Genesis 1:28, God tells them to be fruitful and multiply and to take care of His creation.

When Adam and Eve heard these commands, what do you think their reaction was? Do you think that they felt panicked and overwhelmed? I don't think so. I believe that these commands were easy and natural for them.

Why do I believe this? Let's look at what happens after Adam and Eve sinned in the beginning of Genesis Chapter 3. God responds by giving them consequences for their actions in v. 16-18. To Eve, He says that childbirth *will now be* painful and difficult. He then tells Adam that working the ground *will be* painful toil.

What can we conclude from the consequences that God doles out? The logical conclusion is that before sin came on the scene, childbirth and tending the ground were not intended to be difficult. *If these things were already difficult from the beginning, the consequence God gave in v. 16-18 would be no consequence at all.*

It's clear; God's original intent was for these commands of being fruitful and multiplying (childbirth) and caring for His creation (tending the ground) to be natural. God gave these commands because Adam and Eve were designed to do them. They were created to be fruitful and multiply and to care for His creation.

If you think about it, why should we expect anything different? *Why would God give commands that run counter to how He made Adam and Eve? This would run contrary to His loving nature and being a good, intelligent creator.*

God's commands are supposed to be a reflection of Himself and who He made us to be. Difficulty in following the commands came when sin entered the picture. *Sin marred God's original intent.* What God designed to happen naturally and easily became difficult and more burdensome.

Enter Jesus. Jesus came to restore God's original intent for us. He came to take care of the sin problem. Without sin's hold on us, we can now return to God's initial design for His people.

The commands in the Bible are a description of who He made His people to be. They are not supposed to be a heavy weight or hoops to jump through. They are not supposed to difficult. They are supposed to be easy and light (see Matthew 11:28-30).

This is a huge shift in thinking, especially having grown up with PBT. Can we view the commands as a description of who God made and recreated us to be instead of things on our "to-do lists?" This is the challenge we face.

THAT'S WHAT WE ARE MADE FOR

Because seeing God's commands in this way represents such a major shift in thinking, let's look at one more passage that sheds more light. It's found in Ephesians 2:8-10:

> [8] For it is by grace you have been saved, through faith—and this is not from yourselves, it is the gift of God— [9] not by works, so that no one can boast. [10] For we are God's handiwork, created in Christ Jesus to do good works, which God prepared in advance for us to do.

This is an interesting passage. It talks about grace (as opposed to works) in v. 8 and 9 and in the very next verse it says that we are to do good works (v. 10). Which one is it? Is it not about doing good works or *is it* about doing good works?

If we view doing good works as performance or earning, then this passage becomes muddy. However, when we examine v. 10 more closely, things become clearer.

When we read v. 10, our minds tend to go straight to the part where we are supposed to do "good works, which God prepared in advance for us to do." Maybe it's because we are conditioned to focus on our performance, but it's easy to gloss over the first part of the verse, which is the most important part.

Paul says that *"we are God's handiwork, created in Christ Jesus to do good works"* (v. 10, emphasis mine). Did you catch that? We are made FOR good works. This is part of our DNA and how God designed us. Paul recognizes that because of God's grace (v. 8, 9), we have been restored to God's original specifications for our life.

Doing good works is not abnormal. It's not something that we have to force ourselves to do. It's not something that we have to grow into. It's not something that we have to discipline and train ourselves to do. It's what we were created for!

The discipline comes in training our thinking. The training should not be directed toward our actions. It needs to be aimed at our thinking which affects our experience of the things we do. It's our PBT that causes what should be normal and enjoyable to be burdensome and heavy.

It's when we fail to recognize this truth that we spend our energy trying to train ourselves to become something that we are naturally designed for.

CLIMBING MOUNT EVEREST

The Bible says that we are supposed to love our neighbor as ourselves (Mark 12:31). Is our initial reaction to this command to question how we measure up? Do we do an assessment of how loving we've been?

And if we haven't been loving, then do we feel like we better step it up? When we see someone in need, do we feel the pressure and obligation that we have to love them? Do we think that's what a good Christian *should* do?

On the contrary, we need to see loving people as a natural outflow of who we are. We need to see that it's not something that we have to become, but it's already a part of who we are in Christ. It's normal. It's natural. It's part of our new identity. It's not a burden.

Remember 2 Corinthians 5:17(ESV):

> Therefore, if anyone is in Christ, he is a new creation. The old has passed away; behold, the new has come.

As we see from this verse, our new identity as Christians is found *in Christ.* Is Christ's nature loving? Is this part of who He is or is it something that He had to become through hard work and striving? The answer is clearly the former.

Our new identity is found in Christ. We have been recreated to be in His image. We, like Jesus, are also designed to be loving. It's part of our new nature.

By contrast, when we have the wrong starting point (that we are not loving), we place ourselves at the bottom of a huge mountain to climb. We feel the expectations and guilt for not being more loving instead of feeling secure in the fact that our new nature is already loving by God's design.

When we are overloaded with things to do in our lives, going up this steep mountain seems daunting and overwhelming. It feels like we are trying to climb Mount Everest, *and this is just one command.*

As I mentioned, there are hundreds of other commands in the Bible. Do you see how easily these commands can become a burden when we think that we need to climb *all* those mountains? On the flip side, it is wonderful and freeing to see that God has already placed us on each mountaintop with Christ to enjoy the view.

It all starts with the right perspective and thinking. We need to clear out the wrong thinking about our performance, and we need to make room to interject the correct thinking. In order to help us make this transition, let's look at a couple of practical examples.

DIRTY DISHES

In my household, we have a division of labor. Each person has certain roles they play to keep things running. My wife is the primary person who cooks the meals. My son takes out the trash. My daughter helps take care of the dogs. My job? To do the dishes and clean the toilets. Yay!

I would gladly trade my job for one of the other jobs. But this is the one that fell into my lap. Even though these are not difficult tasks, they felt burdensome. I didn't like doing them. I often put them off until the sink was overflowing with dishes or the toilets were looking and smelling really awful.

To make things worse, when I was obtaining my value from what my wife thought about me, this added more pressure to get these things done. I could feel the weight from my PBT while doing these tasks. I would do them with a horrible attitude. When I did them, I would be a like a little child who feels the need to *specifically* point out to my wife that I had cleared the dishes or cleaned the bathrooms.

Why did I feel the need to show my wife what I had done? Because I needed her affirmation. I needed to relieve the pressure of wondering if she was pleased with me. Unfortunately, it was just feeding into my PBT.

One Saturday afternoon, after God had helped me significantly break the hold of PBT in my life, something strange happened. I was in the kitchen doing the dishes and I found myself ENOYING IT!

I was singing and worshipping God while doing the dishes and found myself feeling joyful. It was hard for me to believe, considering how much I loathed washing the dishes.

On that day, I came to realize that I am already a good father and a good husband. That's who I am. I didn't have to strive to become that. I didn't have to climb the "good husband" mountain and scale the "good father" mountaintop. I am already those things. That's who God made and recreated me to be.

I felt free on that day. I realized I didn't have to work so hard. I didn't have to prove myself to my wife or my kids that I am a good husband or father. It transformed how I viewed and experienced doing things around the house.

Now, I wash dishes and clean toilets while worshipping God because I like things clean. I do them naturally because I'm a good husband and father. I enjoy this much more than before because I don't carry my PBT and have replaced it with the proper way God would have me see myself. The result is that my experience doing these household chores has drastically changed.

Full disclosure: I am not joyfully running around the house cleaning all the time. Sometimes it is a CHORE, but when it feels this way, I often recognize it's because I am carrying the 150-lb. backpack. As a result, I'm feeling so tired and exhausted that it makes doing these household duties too much.

At these times, I have to remain steadfast and not return to my old way of thinking. I simply need to course correct. I need to realign my thinking and reset myself.

When I do, I can move forward with a better perspective. When I do, I find myself doing the dishes and maybe even doing other peoples' duties too. *Having God's way of thinking about yourself and what you do makes all the difference in the world.*

A BETTER SON-IN-LAW

Harry recounted this story to me when we were meeting together and learning about how to leave behind our performance-based thinking. In this story, Harry shared how he was having a difficult time with his in-laws.

Whenever he, his wife and two kids would get together with his wife's family, his in-laws would often criticize him on the decisions he was making. His in-laws would point out ways he was not being a good husband to their daughter. The implication was clear: he was not a good son-in-law.

This did not sit well with my friend. Harry is a well-educated and capable person. He is very successful and hard working. Hearing these critiques about his performance as a son-in-law were difficult to receive.

After reaching a boiling point, he would sometimes blow up at his in-laws. He would yell and argue with them. Afterwards, he would feel terrible about how he reacted and confessed this to God. But no matter how hard he tried to make his in-laws happy, the cycle would repeat itself. Then God began to show him a different perspective.

God revealed that Harry was *already* a good son-in-law. He wasn't a good son-in-law because of his performance, it was because of Harry's new nature in Christ. Part of his new nature was to be a good son-in-law. This changed everything.

Harry stopped *striving to become* something that was already part of his new nature. You know what happened next? He naturally starting acting like a good son-in-law! He found himself doing things a good son-in-law would do. Some of what he was doing was the same as before, but with a different attitude.

Some of what he was doing was new and surprising to him. God was revealing things that Harry had never thought of before. It all came as a result of changing his mindset. *When he had a different starting point (being a good son-in-law), he was in a better position to hear from God and live out his new identity.*

Do you see what happened? Without having to climb this huge mountain to become a good son-in-law and without the guilt-bearing, heavy-laden thinking from his PBT, he was free to be who God recreated him to be. With the correct view of his performance as a good son-in-law, God naturally led him to do the things that he was designed to do.

SOLID GROUND

One of the byproducts of PBT is that it creates insecurity and uncertainty in our lives. In the story with Harry, how much would he need to do to feel secure that he was indeed a good son-in-law? How much is enough? No matter how much he would do, there would always be the feeling that he *could* have been doing more.

When we have our identity based on performance, what we do will never be enough. We will always have a nagging sense of insecurity. We will constantly struggle with the uncertainty over whether we've done enough.

When we see our identity through the lens of our performance instead of the lens of our Creator, we will never feel secure. We will constantly be carrying the 150-lb backpack while scaling the mountains in our lives.

All this is exhausting and leads to burnout. Worse than that, all this is unnecessary. It is unnecessary because of Jesus. When He died for our sins and recreated us, we have our identity in Him, not in what we do.

We need to shift our footing to solid ground. We must ground our identity in something that's not fleeting and unstable, like our performance. We need to find our identity in Christ.

If you've grown up in the church, you've probably heard that before. But we will see how shifting our thinking can help us see this truth from a different perspective. We will see that without PBT, our identity in Christ won't be simply head knowledge.

This is our next stop in Phase C. Before we do, spend some time reflecting on this chapter.

===

WHAT ABOUT MY LIFE?

1. Why do you think it's difficult for us to separate our identity from what we do?

2. What mountains do you find yourself trying to climb? Describe the weight and burden of feeling like you need to *become* a good mother, good Christian, good son, be more loving, etc.

3. Imagine what it would be like to stop striving to become something God already recreated you to be in Christ. How would your life be different?

CHAPTER 11

TRUE IDENTITY

WHO AM I NOW?

After breaking our PBT boulders, we will be in a good place. It's a good place because we will start experiencing freedom and relief. Freedom from the hold and influence of our performance and the expectation of others. We will have relief from the heavy weight we were constantly carrying and the anti-fruit that accompanied it.

But once we become free from our old way of deriving our value and identity, we will face other questions. Who am I now? What do I do now that I'm free? How do I think about myself? After having performance and others drive me for so long, what is my driving force?

In this chapter and the next, we will cover these questions. First, let's address the questions about who we are and how we should be viewing ourselves. Since we don't have the boulders clouding our thinking, we are now free to see ourselves the way that God sees us. Let's look at the list below that describes how God sees us and our new identity.

WHO I AM IN CHRIST

I am God's Child (Jn 1:12)

I am joint heirs with Christ (Rom 8:17)

I am forgiven (Col 1:13,14)

I am alive with Christ (Eph 2:4,5)

I am a new creation (2 Cor 5:17)

I am the light of the world (Matt 5:14)

I am the temple of the Holy Spirit (1 Cor 6:19)

I am the salt of the earth (Matt 5:13)

I am blessed (Gal 3:9)

I am the righteousness of God (2 Cor 5:21)

I am a saint (Rom 1:7 - NIV uses holy people)

I am chosen (1 Thess 1:4)

I am holy and without blame (Eph 1:4)

I am God's workmanship (Eph 2:10)

I am elect (1 Pet 1:1)

I am beloved (Col 3:12)

I am victorious (Rev 21:7)

I am Christ's friend (John 15:15)

I am set free (Gal 5:1; John 8:32)

I am one with God in spirit (1 Cor 6:17)

I am more than a conqueror (Rom 8:37)

I am adopted into God's family (Gal 4:4-7)

These are the truths detailing who we are as Christians. This is the solid foundation that we will build upon in this new season of life. During this season, we need to consistently declare the truths found in this list.

To help incorporate this, we can use this list when we practice the Reflection Tool (Chapters 8 and 9). When we make an exchange (Step 4), we can ask God to show us from this list how He see us in the various situations we are experiencing.

In Phase C, we will continue abandoning our old PBT identity, but as we do, we must now exchange it for our true identity. *If we rid ourselves of our faulty foundation but don't replace it with a new foundation, we will have nothing to stand on!*

DO I REALLY BELIEVE?

Take a look at this list again. This time ask yourself the question, "Do I really believe this is true about myself?" The test to see if you really believe is to ask yourself, "If this is *actually* true about myself, what *difference* is it making in my life?"

For example, if I'm God's son, that should be impacting my daily life. How would I think and act differently if I was a child of God? If God, who is over the whole universe, is my Father, shouldn't that fact change me and my life? If I've embraced this truth, it certainly should.

If I allow myself to fully embrace that I'm a child of God, I should feel safe and secure. My security comes from the fact that my Father is the king and I'm his child. And if that's true, then I should carry myself differently.

If my Father is so powerful, I shouldn't be as concerned when people are coming against me. If my Father is powerful and loves me, then I should be confident He will take care of all my needs. If He is taking care of all my needs, I shouldn't feel the need to control everything.

When I find myself *trying* to control my kids' actions, I'm not acting like a child of God. If I'm trying to take control of my finances or my job or my circumstances, I'm acting more like an orphan trying to protect what I have, than a son or daughter of the King.

If I'm a child of God, I would know that I am loved. I would feel secure and not try to gain everyone's approval. Since I am loved, I would be free to now love others. Because I feel fulfilled, I can now think about the needs of others without being so concerned with my needs. If I am a child of God, it should make a difference!

When we look at this list of who we are in Christ, we can't let these truths be simply head knowledge that make no impact in our lives. *If we think about the PBT boulders, we can see how these made a significant impact in our everyday lives. Shouldn't our new identity in Christ have just as much of an impact in our post-PBT lives?*

Let's look at the following example to see why it might be difficult for us to fully embrace our new identity.

I'M A SAINT! . . . REALLY?

I was attending a seminar about our new identity in Christ. In the material they had a list similar to what's included here. They had us review this and rate from 1 (being not at all) to 5 (being very well) how these descriptions matched what we thought about ourselves. My results surprised me.

I had a few 4's and 5's, but I also had a lot of 1's and 2's. I was sharing my results with a friend and she exclaimed, "Aren't you the one who taught classes about our identity in Christ?" I knew what she was thinking because I was thinking the same thing. How did I know and teach these truths but not believe them for myself?

Then I realized what the problem was. Because I had based who I was on my performance for so long, I had trouble shifting my thinking to start believing these truths were actually true about me apart from what I do.

For example, the Bible mentions numerous times that part of our new identity is that we are now saints. Now, what comes to mind when you think about a "saint"? Perfect? Holy? Someone who walks on water? Now when you look at your life, do you really measure up to this? Can you, with all honesty, call yourself a saint?

And if you do say that you are a saint, what is your reason for believing this is true? Do you feel like your life matches that of a saint? Or would you think that you are a hypocrite if you ever declared this about yourself?

This is the problem that I faced during the seminar I was attending. Even though God had started freeing me from the influence of PBT, I still couldn't accept that I was a saint or holy. PBT was still influencing how I viewed myself. I still had more adjusting to do in my thinking.

If we base our acceptance of being a saint on our actions, we will never feel comfortable embracing this truth about who we are. How can we ever feel right declaring that we are saints if we see sin in our lives? If we are not living like saints, will we ever be confident and secure in our new identity?

The answer is you cannot and will not be able to do this. We have to adjust our thinking and move away from being performance-based. We have to see that our identity and who we are is based on what God has done, not on what we are doing.

We can't let our failure or inability to live out our new character make us doubt who we really are. God made this change in us. *We have to understand and accept that it's going to take time for our thinking, actions and feelings to "catch up" to the truth about who we are.*

ROYALTY

Imagine if one day, you received a letter in the mail. The letter shares that you had a distant uncle who just passed away. Your uncle was actually the king of a small country in the South Pacific and he didn't have any children of his own. The government officially began searching for any living relative. They finally found you.

After realizing this is not a scam, you are overjoyed. They send a private jet to come pick you up. You are now going to be the leader of this small nation. You arrive and they take you to the palace that you will now call home.

Then reality sets in. You have NO IDEA what you are doing. You are making mistakes left and right. You don't know how to act like royalty. You don't know how to carry yourself. You don't how royalty thinks. You have to learn how to dress differently. You have to learn how to eat with three different forks. You have to learn how to address people properly.

Now, does the fact that you don't know how to live like royalty make you not royalty? Of course, it doesn't. You just have to spend time training yourself to think and act like who you are now.

This is a picture of how we should think about our new identity in Christ. In fact, the Bible says we are indeed royalty. 1 Peter 2:9 says that we are a "chosen people" and a "royal priesthood." But going from a commoner to royalty will require us to go through an adjustment period. We have to give ourselves time to adjust to our new identity.

OUT OF CHARACTER

When we sin and fail, we can't allow doubt to seep in. We can't look at our failures and conclude that we are not saints. Instead, we need to see that we are acting out of character.

That is the way to view sin as Christians. *Sin is not evidence against our new identity as saints and righteous ones. It's evidence that we are acting out of character and we need time to adjust our thinking.*

The solution? Start acting like a new creation. Start the process of learning what that means. In the beginning of the process, you won't know how to do that. That is not only ok, it's expected!

Remember, this is not positive thinking. It's aligning our behavior with the reality of what God did in recreating us. It's not tricking ourselves to believe something that is not true. It's true because God made this change within us.

Let's use another "royal" example to depict what we are talking about: take King Henry. King Henry is an established and respected king. One day, he decides that he wants to leave his palace and go beg in the streets. As the king, he has every right to be able to do this if he chooses.

He could exit his castle and throw his robe and crown in the trash. He could then go on the street corner and beg for money and food. But once he recognizes that this is not for him, *all he has to do is go back* to the castle and put on his spare robe and crown.

He just has to go back to being who he truly is and was all along. Even when he was begging on the street corner, he was still a king. He was just acting out of character. The solution wouldn't be to get a job and work his way back up the ladder. The solution is remembering that he is a king and to start acting like one.

PRINCES AND PRINCESSES

The same is true for us spiritually. As we saw in 1 Peter 2:9, we are royalty. *Because our Father is the King and we are His children, that makes us princes and princesses.* But we can still choose to exit the throne room and go beg on the street. We can choose to sin and separate ourselves from the King. We need to recognize that what we are doing is not in alignment with who we are. We are acting out of character.

The solution is not to work harder so we feel worthy of being sons or daughters of the King. What we do doesn't make us princes and princesses. We are royalty because our Father is the King. We will *never merit this high position.*

Our standing doesn't come from our performance and it never will. This standing comes from God making a fundamental change in who we are and our identity. It comes from Him, not from us.

We need to see that if we base our new identity on our performance, we will NEVER be able to accept, embrace and be secure in who God says we are. If we base being a royal priesthood or being a saint on our performance, how could we ever measure up? When would we ever be comfortable saying this about ourselves? We need to break this false connection between who we are and what we do.

As Christians, we aren't saints because we don't sin. We are saints because Jesus never sinned and our new identity is found in Him. We are saints because God changed who we are based on Christ's work, not ours. We can't change the script and base how we feel about ourselves on our own doing.

Our performance is a byproduct of who we are, not a determiner of who we are in Christ. Unless we make this switch in our thinking, we will always feel insecure. We will never be confident in our new identity because our performance will never measure up to the high standing we have in Christ.

Only Christ's work will measure up to this lofty position that we have. We have to see it, believe it, receive it and praise Him for it. *We need to stop letting our failure to <u>live out and experience</u> our new identity make us doubt who we are. It's trusting in who we are and what God has done that <u>produces the right behavior.</u>*

We need to thank God that we are righteous, even if our actions haven't caught up to our new identity. We need to accept that we are royalty, no matter how uncomfortable that makes us feel. We need to fully embrace that we are unconditionally loved sons and daughters. When we do, our actions will come in line with the truth.

Make these declarations! Declare that you are who God says you are, not what your performance or other people say you are. Affirm these truths daily. This is the flip side of getting rid of our performance-based identity. It's making an exchange for a more solid foundation.

As we close this chapter, I want to emphasize one more thing about our new identity. There is one critical element of our new identity that we need so we can proceed to our final destination of Phase C.

HE LIKES ME, HE REALLY LIKES ME

If we are God's children, not only does He love us, we must see that He *likes* us, too. When we read that God loves us, we might get a picture of Him enduring, long suffering, and putting up with us in order to do so. But this is not true. God likes us and chooses to be with us.

In Genesis Chapter 1, God created the earth, plants and animals on days one through five. On day six, He had a choice. He could have just enjoyed His creation, which He thought was "good," by Himself or He could have created mankind. Even though God is a complete community of Father, Son and Holy Spirit, He chose to create mankind anyway.

What does that tell us? Instead of choosing to be alone, He favored being with us. He knew ahead of time that we'd mess up (see Genesis chapter 3 and beyond) and cause havoc. But He chose to create mankind anyway, because God wants to be with us that much.

It's the picture of the prodigal son story we recounted. The father is *running* to be with us and throws a party because we're reunited with Him. Does that sound like someone who is simply tolerating us? Or does that sound like someone who genuinely likes to be with us? *God is not with us not out of obligation. He WANTS to be with us because He likes us!*

As we look at our new identity, we need to allow our thinking to adjust. Having been based on performance, our perspective is off base. We have to make the appropriate adjustments. God is for us. God is not waiting for us to get it all together. God thinks the world of us. That's why He sent His son Jesus to die for us.

Still having a hard time believing that God really values you that much?

MILLION-DOLLAR SHACK

Let's say you own a tiny 300 sq. ft. one-room house with giant holes in the walls and a roof that is on the verge of collapsing. This house is smack in the middle of the worst neighborhood with the highest crime rate in your city. You decide that you've had enough of this and put your house up for sale.

You meet with your realtor. She asks if you want to put your house on the market. You tell her that you do and want to list your house for $1 million. Your agent tries her best to contain herself but she thinks you are crazy!

She goes on to tell you that you can't list your house for that amount because it's not worth that much. You go on to tell her that you grew up in this house and it's been in your family for five generations. Your agent doesn't seem moved at all.

She asks you, "Do you know how they assess the value of a house?" She continues to educate you that they assess the value of a house by looking at what other people were willing to pay for houses similar to yours.

The Principle: *Value is determined by what someone is willing to pay.*

Now, if value is determined by what someone is willing to pay, what does that say about your value? What was God willing to pay for you? He paid the highest price possible. He sacrificed His one and only Son, who has eternal, *infinite value.*

What does that say about how much God values you? Don't gloss over this question. Pause. Take a moment to consider the answer and the implications. Think about how deeply He must love you in order to pay such a high price for you.

Now consider this follow-up question. Does that match how you see yourself and how valuable you think you are? And if not, what needs to change?

Does God need to adjust His assessment of you? Does He need to come to His senses and realize that He bought a lemon and got ripped off when He purchased you? Or do *we need to change?*

We need to stop believing the performance-based lie that we are nothing and no one and start agreeing with God. We are valuable, much more than we allow ourselves to accept.

What God was willing to pay in exchange for us is proof of our extraordinary value. We must not let our achievements, or lack thereof, convince us that this is not true about ourselves.

The good news? We can do this. We can make this change. Without our PBT lens on, we *can* see ourselves this way. Take one final look at the list about our identity in Christ and when you do, ask yourself, "If these truths were *NOT based on my ability or circumstance*, could I believe this is true about myself?

WHO I AM IN CHRIST

I am God's Child (Jn 1:12)

I am forgiven (Col 1:13,14)

I am a new creation (2 Cor 5:17)

I am the temple of the Holy Spirit (1 Cor 6:19)

I am blessed (Gal 3:9)

I am a saint (Rom 1:7 - NIV uses holy people)

I am holy and without blame (Eph 1:4)

I am elect (1 Pet 1:1)

I am victorious (Rev 21:7)

I am set free (Gal 5:1; John 8:32)

I am more than a conqueror (Rom 8:37)

I am joint heirs with Christ (Rom 8:17)

I am alive with Christ (Eph 2:4,5)

I am the light of the world (Matt 5:14)

I am the salt of the earth (Matt 5:13)

I am the righteousness of God (2 Cor 5:21)

I am chosen (1 Thess 1:4)

I am God's workmanship (Eph 2:10)

I am beloved (Col 3:12)

I am Christ's friend (John 15:15)

I am one with God in spirit (1 Cor 6:17)

I am adopted into God's family (Gal 4:4-7)

I hope you are starting to see that it's possible to step into your new identity without hesitation or feeling like a hypocrite. You can use your newfound freedom to believe and declare these truths about who you are.

You can recognize that your sin and failure are simply acting out of character. You can repent and then turn back to who you really are. Our mistakes don't exist to condemn us and make us doubt our true identity in Christ. Instead, our sin is evidence that we need to adjust our thinking and start believing what God and the Bible says about who we are. Then start acting like it.

BEFORE WE CROSS THE FINISH LINE

Before we discuss what ultimate freedom looks like, I want to implore you one last time. In order to move forward in Phase C, you cannot overlook this very important step of believing how valued and loved you are. It's foundational; I have to go back to drink from this well time and time again.

We must have an unshakeable assurance that God loves us. We have to declare it, depend on it, bask in it and enjoy it. We need to feel satisfied by it, changed by it, and driven by it. This will provide the security needed to go onto the next step.

Don't shortchange yourself. Once you break free from PBT, you put yourself in prime position to start receiving God's grace and being loved *unconditionally*. Take full advantage. Receive what God has ALREADY given you. He's waiting for you to do so.

His love is agape, unconditional love. God doesn't know how to love any other way. If we can't receive unconditionally, it's no wonder that we are love starved. But here's the good part. Since our spiritual stomachs are empty, we can eat and eat and not get full, so enjoy God to the fullest!

Declare it in the morning. Declare it when you pray for your meal. Declare it before you do your quiet time and when you pray. God loves you for you. *God loves you because you are His sons and daughters. There is no other reason.*

This is what we've longed for our entire lives. This is what we wished we could have experienced more of from our parents and family. This is what we're created for. This is what we now have because of Jesus.

WHAT ABOUT MY LIFE?

1. Go back and look at the Who I Am In Christ chart. Ask God to highlight one of those descriptions of who we are. Then ask yourself, what difference would it make if you really, truly believed this was true. How would it change your parenting, your reactions at work or school, your fears, your worries, your stress, etc.?

2. Describe how you view yourself and how valuable you think you are. Is this based on your performance or what others think of you? If so, spend some time using the Repentance Tool. Repent of this false way of thinking. Invite Jesus to come be present with you. Ask Him to exchange the way you see yourself with a new way.

CHAPTER 12

ULTIMATE FREEDOM

This is the end game. This is the goal that we've been pursuing. It's for us to experience ultimate freedom, the final aspect of Phase C.

But before examining our final destination, let's pause and review where we've traveled so far.

Here's a recap of where we've gone:

- We've identified how PBT is ever present in our lives (Phase A).

- We've used anti-fruit as road signs to help identify and address the PBT boulders blocking our path (Phase A).

- We've armed ourselves with two tools (Repentance and Reflection) that we can use on a daily basis to rid ourselves of this virus in our lives (Phase B).

- We've looked at the right way of thinking about our performance and the commands in the Bible (Phase C).

- We've seen how vital it is to put on our new identity, especially being beloved (Phase C).

Now, we'll close our journey by looking at what ultimate freedom looks like. We get a good picture of this in John 5:19-20:

> [19] Jesus gave them this answer: "Very truly I tell you, the Son can do nothing by himself; he can do only what he sees his Father doing, because whatever the Father does the Son also does. [20] For the Father loves the Son and shows him all he does. Yes, and he will show him even greater works than these, so that you will be amazed.

What is ultimate freedom? It's total submission to our Father. It's the life that Jesus lived. He lived *freer* than any other person that ever walked this planet. He completely submitted His will to the will of His Father. He boldly claimed that the "Son can do *nothing* by himself, He can do only what He sees His Father doing (emphasis mine)."

This is the penultimate freedom that we can experience—to let God do everything! It was His plan from the beginning that we do nothing on our own initiative. Freedom is found in His Spirit leading us and directing us through His word. *Ultimate freedom is not being driven by ourselves, circumstances, or others but by the One who loves us and knows us perfectly.*

Ultimate freedom will be found when we completely abandon a performance-driven life. When we have no more desire to achieve things on our own for ourselves, we will really be free.

SPIRIT LED

When we give up total control to our Father, we give His Spirit permission to take the driver's seat. As long as we have our hands on the wheel (because PBT won't let us release our death grip), we will never experience the freedom found in God's Spirit moving and working in us. When we have a clear sense of God's presence and His Spirit, this is where we'll find true life and joy.

As long as we depend on our own performance, we'll never be free to experience the fruit of the Spirit on a regular basis (see Galatians 5:22-23). But once we leave our PBT behind, the Spirit has room to operate. *He can accomplish things that we never fathomed, hoped or imagined.*

Matthew 13:8 talks about what happens when seed (the gospel) takes root in "good soil." The verse says that the crop yields thirty-, sixty- or one-hundred-fold. On our own, we could be satisfied with a 10% or 20% return. God's Spirit produces astronomical, non-human, miraculous returns of 3,000%, 6,000% or 10,000%. This type of return cannot be gained from our own effort but only by God's power.

This is the playground of Phase C and ultimate freedom. We listen and follow God's prompting and then enjoy the fruit that goes beyond human comprehension and understanding. We take this tiny step in faith, and God responds by producing twelve overflowing basketfuls of oversized fruit in our lives (see John 6:1-13).

LOST IN TRANSLATION

In 2014, I took a team to India. We were there to teach the concepts in this book. My friend Zachery had a ministry in India which taught and encouraged local pastors. He wanted me to share about ridding ourselves of PBT and receiving our new identity in Christ.

I was excited about this opportunity but also a bit nervous. I didn't know how this material would translate to the culture in India. I knew how it applied in the United States but didn't know if it was as applicable across the world.

The first church I visited was in a city that had a lot of professionals who were proficient in English. I was relieved that I didn't need a translator. As I began teaching, I soon realized that everything I was sharing was hitting home. They related to my stories and the truths about PBT.

I discovered that these truths are universal. It wasn't just in the United States that people perceived their value came from their performance and others' view of them.

Next, I visited another church in a countryside village. Our driver took us along a dirt road and then stopped in the middle of nowhere. He told us to get out and start walking up a huge hill. We walked for what seemed like forever to the top of the mountainside. The church met on this mountaintop to avoid persecution.

This church was drastically different from the first church in the city. The group was mostly women who were very poor and uneducated. They did not speak any English, so this time I had to work with a translator. They also couldn't read, so I had to throw out all my written material.

I started to teach and share the same material that I have given hundreds of times before. I knew the material so well; it was all done by memory. It didn't take long before I realized that the women weren't connecting with what I was sharing.

I turned to my translator and asked, "Do you think they understand what I'm teaching?" He turned to me and shook his head "no." I didn't know what to do. I couldn't use my written material. They couldn't understand what I was sharing.

I prayed, "God help me!" Suddenly God gave me an idea of how to change my lesson. I went on to share my material using totally different examples that I had never used before. I started seeing eyes light up and the women nodding their heads in agreement.

After the lesson, the women split into small groups to discuss what we had just learned. In all the groups, the women were weeping and sobbing. I asked my translator what was happening. He told me that God was revealing how PBT was affecting them and the pain it was causing in their lives and families. We began to pray and minister to them. I could see they were being transformed.

I was in awe of what God did in that moment. He revealed insight in a way I could have *never* accomplished on my own. I couldn't rely on what I had prepared. I couldn't lean on my own understanding or past experience.

God was in control and He was rewriting my material in real time. He used the new stories to touch those women's hearts. Our team joined together to praise God for what He had done.

The women experienced freedom on that day but I also experienced freedom too. I was freed from relying on my knowledge and training. I was freed to embrace God's leading.

I was the supporting cast. I was doing the work, but it really wasn't me. Words were coming out of my mouth, but I had no idea of exactly where it was going. But God did. And the fruit we experienced that day was beyond what I could have ever envisioned.

POWERING UP

After we had finished teaching in the village, we headed back down the mountain to a guest house. It was a Saturday and the next day we were going to a local church in the area.

Word got out that a team from the United States was visiting. My friend Zachery, who was arranging our itinerary, was suddenly inundated with requests for us to visit. Our original plan was thrown out the window. Instead of going to one church, our team was split up to attend four different churches.

Zachery didn't know which church I was going to attend and give a message. He was having a hard time choosing which churches we would be visiting and which group members would be assigned to the four churches. This was a problem for me because the churches were all so different. Was I going to a church like one in the village or like one in the city?

I had prepared a message beforehand, but I didn't know if this was going to fit the church audience I was going to speak to. I went to sleep still not knowing. In the morning, Zachery came into my room and told me that I was going to visit a small house church in a Muslim neighborhood.

At the house church I met the pastor, William. He greeted me and I sat on the floor as the service was ready to begin. As William was speaking, I looked around at the people gathered there. I was getting a strong sense that the message I had prepared was not going to connect with this group.

I immediately began to pray! I was willing to throw out the message I'd prepared, if God would give me something else to share. I prayed and prayed, but I was receiving nothing. Panic started setting in. I declared that my value didn't come from this message that I was about to give!

Since I didn't receive anything different from God, I began delivering the message I had prepared ahead of time. But as I started preaching, God started changing my message as I was talking! He was taking over again!

Much like my teaching time at the village church, God was orchestrating my words. I could tell from the expression on everyone's faces that they were fully engaged.

As I was speaking, I started noticing that I felt different. I had never felt this much power and authority as I did when I spoke that day. I become more bold as my message continued. At one point I had everyone stand up and declare some truths about who they were.

I had never done anything like that with as much power and conviction. As I was doing this, tears were flowing down this elderly woman's face. As I continued, more people were crying and declaring out loud what God had done for them.

After the service ended, Pastor William thanked me repeatedly for speaking to his church. I hugged the members of the church as they thanked me too. God had truly met them on that day.

While on my way back to the guest house, I was overjoyed. I praised God for what He had done. Not only did I feel a sense of freedom during the service, I felt a sense of power and authority. The result? People's hearts, minds and spirits were touched by God in a significant way.

This is ultimate freedom. When we are not limited by what we can do, we will be free to experience what God can do in and through us. I experienced a taste of that on this trip to India.

I also experienced similar things back home. I experienced freedom in letting go in ways that were not as dramatic as it was in India.

I've allowed God to "take over" at home while talking to my children when they were struggling. I've had God take the reins when I'm supporting a friend who was hurting. I've had God take the wheel when I'm in a meeting at church and direct it in a way I would have never thought of on my own.

God transformed normal, everyday situations into extraordinary moments.

HOMELESS AND HOMEWARD BOUND

My whole life I've loved sports and being active. Growing up I played volleyball, basketball, baseball and tennis. As I got into my forties, I started to take up running.

Not to insult *actual* runners, I should correct myself. I like to *jog*! When I would go out jogging, I loved to listen to worship music. It was just me and God on the open road.

One late afternoon, I laced up my shoes and took my phone to go jogging. I was jogging on a street near my house listening to worship music. I was really enjoying my time when I came up to a big hill.

As I went down this steep decline, I felt like I was flying. I actually had my arms straight out to the side imagining I had wings. Yes, this was post-PBT when I didn't care what people thought about me! I felt so free and joyful.

As I was approaching the bottom of the hill, I was singing a song called "Oh Happy Day." I thought this was so perfect because that's exactly how I felt. I was so happy being outside and jogging/flying with God. Suddenly, something caught my attention.

Out of the corner of my eye, I saw someone on a bench. He was a homeless man, slouched over. He did not look happy. In fact, he looked very despondent.

I thought to myself there was such a huge contrast between what I was feeling and what this man appeared to be feeling. Ordinarily, I would have continued on my way, but that day God stopped me in my tracks. I sensed He wanted me to go approach this man.

You need to understand that this is not the norm for me. Even though I'm a pastor, I'm much more comfortable in front of a classroom teaching a Bible study than approaching a stranger on the street. I'm a natural introvert and it's a struggle talking to people I don't know.

In the past, I would have sensed that nudging from God and rationalized it away. I would have thought, "What am I going to do if I stop and approach this man? What would I say to him? I don't have anything to give him."

However, this day was different. I didn't worry about not knowing what to do. I just took it one step at a time. The first step was to just stop, so I stopped jogging. Next, I turned around.

As *soon* as I turned around, immediately the homeless man locked eyes with me. This man's name was Oscar. He called me over to sit with him. God was taking control. I knew I just had to listen.

I sat with him and he asked me if I had a dime because he was thirsty and wanted to get a drink. I thought that was odd because you can't buy anything these days for a dime! I told him that I didn't have my wallet because I was out jogging. I wished I had my wallet because I would have gladly bought him a drink. I genuinely felt this.

No sooner did I share this, when the man proceeded to ask me where I lived. I told him that I had been jogging for a while and that I lived a couple of miles away. Then he said, "Let's go back to your house so that you can get your wallet." God had the steering wheel and He was turning this car!

We started walking back up the hill that I had so much fun going down. As we were walking, Oscar started sharing with me that he had just gotten out of prison. I didn't have the courage to ask him what he did. Next, he started speaking in Spanish. I took two years of Spanish in high school, but I had no idea what he was saying.

Then he switched back to English. I could tell he was very disturbed. He kept mentioning that he had done something that he regretted but he wouldn't say what it was. I could sense God prompting me to ask him about it, so I did.

Oscar was hesitant at first to share, but then he went on to tell me about his friend. He and his friend had gone into business together, but his friend ended up stealing money from him. When Oscar confronted him, his friend pulled out a knife and tried to stab Oscar. Oscar wrestled the knife away and then killed his friend.

This was the reason that he was sent to jail. He had just finished a ten-year sentence, but this event was still heavy on his mind and heart.

We made it up this big hill, when he asked me how much further it was to my house. I told him that it was about another mile and a half. Oscar was visibly discouraged and told me to forget it. He turned to go back down the hill. I stopped him and asked him if I could pray for him. He said yes.

I had no idea what I was going to pray. I had no time to plan it out. Instead, God led me. I started praying about his past, his guilt and his shame. I could tell God was touching him. I asked him if he wanted God to remove this weight he was carrying. He said yes. We prayed and eventually Oscar accepted Christ into his life.

After we finished praying, this man's countenance completely changed. His face went from being downcast to beaming. He hugged me and then walked back down the hill. I told him that I would run back home and meet him back at the bottom of the hill so I could buy him something to drink. He told me he didn't need it anymore.

Oscar was so filled, he didn't need physical food or drink any longer. He went skipping down the hill. He was freed. I was freed. This new freedom in Christ we experienced that day was the byproduct of what God had been doing in me for months. He rid me of my dependence and reliance upon my knowledge and things I could control.

That day, I didn't have control. I didn't know what to do or what to pray. But that was ok. Not only was it ok, it was great. It was exactly what God wanted. He had space to move and room to speak. Without me dictating things, the Holy Spirit could take the lead. When He did, look at the fruit that was produced!

Heaven was rejoicing on that day. The angels were rejoicing on that day. Oscar and I were rejoicing on that day! Oscar had crossed over from death to life. His eternity was changed because my PBT was not in the way of God moving and leading.

I've had many encounters like this since God has taken me on this road to freedom. I've experienced more life, freedom and joy than I have ever experienced before. Transformation is happening for my family, for my church and for me by focusing on doing less on my own. By me doing less, God is doing more.

My prayer is that you would experience more by doing less. Without the constraints of PBT, you can actually receive and believe in your true identity. *Being fully loved and secure, you can let go of control and your own performance.* When you let go of control, you will experience true freedom. The freedom that comes from God taking the reins.

This is ultimate freedom. This is the freedom that comes from the gospel message. This is the freedom that is available for everyone that accepts Jesus's death and resurrection. *This is the freedom that is open to everyone willing to let go of PBT and throw it in the trash for good.* Don't look back. Move forward into true life and freedom!!

[You can use the Bonus Material at the end of the book to help you adjust to your new life in Christ.]

WHAT ABOUT MY LIFE?

1. Have you ever experienced a time where you knew God had taken the reins? You were doing the actions or speaking the words, but you KNOW that it was really God. What kind of fruit came out of that situation?

2. How can you actually do more by doing less? Identify areas where you can give up more control to God and stop relying on your own performance, experience and wisdom. What would it look like to let go and let God take control? What would make it difficult for that to happen?

Final Note: If you are reading this book and **have never accepted Christ and what He's done for you,** I want to invite you to do that right now. There is only one way to experience this new life and freedom. It's as simple as accepting God's invitation to be reborn and become His child. If you are ready to do that, just pray this prayer aloud to God:

> *"God, I know that I have fallen short and sinned throughout my life, but I want to turn to you now. I want to receive what Jesus did for me by paying for my wrongs and dying on a cross. I want to receive new life, because Jesus rose from the dead and came back to life. I want you to take control over my life. Thank you for receiving me. Amen!"*

If you just prayed that prayer, **CONGRATULATIONS!! Welcome to God's family!** You and I are now family members! I want to encourage you to tell someone what you just did in becoming a Christian. Everything written in this book is what it means to be a Christian. The bonus material at the end of the book contains more insight into the Christian life.

Whether you just became a Christian or have been one for fifty years, I want to encourage all of you to read the bonus material found in the last section.

Throughout this book, I intentionally chose many examples from everyday life that most people could relate to. But there are other things unique to the Christian life that might still be unclear for you.

Some might struggle with how they have been raised in the church and how to change their approach towards reading the Bible and prayer.

Topics like this will be found in the pages of the bonus material and give a snapshot of how we can do what God commands while remaining free.

This last section is addressed toward those that may have difficulty fully embracing or applying the principles conveyed in this book. Maybe you grew up in a household or church that put an extremely heavy emphasis on performance. The material in this section will be especially helpful for you.

It is also for those that have accepted these principles but need help adjusting their thinking and life to match. I know I needed help in my post-PBT life. Having lived a certain way for so long, it took God's grace and insight for me to begin to flourish without PBT.

In this section we will address several key areas in our Christian life and in our relationship with God.

SPIRITUAL DISCIPLINES?

Have you ever heard of the term "spiritual disciplines"? It's a term that refers to activities that we can do to help us in our walk with God. These are things like reading the Bible, prayer, fasting, worship, reflection and solitude.

Over the years I've read numerous books about the spiritual disciplines. Often these books focused on making the disciplines a bigger part of our lives. I read these books because, frankly, I needed help. I needed tips on how to be more consistent and make these spiritual activities a regular part of my life.

Then I discovered something about the spiritual disciplines. I realized that one reason I struggled, is the whole idea of spiritual *disciplines* is flawed.

Don't get me wrong, I love the activities of reading the Bible, prayer, worship, etc. I just don't think that we should be calling them *disciplines*. Attaching this label to these wonderful things is misleading.

The word discipline can have the connotation that these spiritual activities are not natural. *The fact that I have to discipline myself to pray makes me think that prayer is something I either don't like to do or that doesn't come naturally to me.* Neither of these could be further from the truth.

As we detailed in one of the earlier chapters, performing all these spiritual disciplines are things that we are designed for. *Why would God command us to pray, unless this was exactly what He had in mind when He created us?*

Prayer or solitude are things that God put into our wiring and are a part of our spiritual DNA. These are not things we need to be disciplining ourselves to do.

For example, prayer is communication with God. It is a time to express our heart to our Heavenly Father and an opportunity for God to express His heart, desire and will to us. Prayer is about our *relationship with God, not a discipline.*

IN THE DOGHOUSE

If I told my wife, "Honey you should be proud of me. I really have disciplined myself to spend time with you. That just shows how much I love you. I denied myself and overcame my inclination to do other things and *trained* myself to talk with you!" How do you think my wife would respond to that? If you said she would throw me into the doghouse, you'd be right.

That's not how I feel about spending time with my wife. That's also not how I feel about time with my Heavenly Father. I don't need to discipline myself to spend time with Him and talk with Him. There's nothing better than being with the One I love more than life itself. This is not something that I have to train myself to do.

Now, it's important that we don't confuse intentionality with disciplining ourselves. In the above example, I *do* need to be intentional about spending time with my wife. I should be intentional about focusing on being who God created me to be. In this case a good, loving husband.

The key is my mindset. Is my starting point that I am not a good husband who needs to discipline and train himself to become one? Am I struggling or striving to be a good husband and be one with my wife? Or is this me being exactly who I am in Christ?

Don't get me wrong, there are things in the world that make it difficult for us to carry out who were created to be (sin, a fallen world, PBT, past hurt etc.). But we cannot be led to the wrong conclusion that we need to change who we are. I am a loving husband even if my circumstances or wrong thinking make it difficult for me to demonstrate it.

THAT JUST CAN'T WORK

I remember speaking to a pastor about this idea of not having to discipline myself to pray. He had difficulty accepting this idea. He insisted that we do need to discipline ourselves to pray. *His underlying thinking is that if we don't discipline ourselves to pray, we won't pray as much as we should or want to do.*

I completely understood where he was coming from. I spent my entire Christian life thinking the same way. I had the same concerns that if I didn't train myself to pray that it just wouldn't happen. Praying just when I felt like praying? Are you kidding? How often would I pray if I didn't spend time and effort disciplining myself to pray?

I realize now that this type of fear and worry comes from our PBT. *Instead of trusting that God recreated us and gave us this innate desire to be with Him, we put our trust in our own effort to make prayer happen.* The byproduct is that we are insecure about our ability or desire to pray.

When I started to change my thinking, it transformed my prayer life. When I began realizing that I didn't have to discipline myself to pray, I was able to see the truth.

I was made for God. I was created to communicate with Him. The result is that I didn't spend time training myself to pray, yet I found myself praying all of the time, throughout the day.

The key question is this: what is empowering you to pray—God's design or your discipline? Do we pray because this is how God created us, or do we learn to do this through making it a habit?

WWJD (WHAT WOULD JESUS DO)

Maybe you're thinking that is just one person's experience. But consider this question: do you think that Jesus had to discipline Himself to pray to His Father? Or do you think that praying and talking with His Father was the most natural thing that Jesus could do?

Jesus didn't pray because He had to. Jesus didn't pray because He forced Himself to. He didn't pray to make sure He hit everything on His prayer list. Praying was not something to do, it was a part of who He was.

No, Jesus didn't have to discipline Himself to pray. He prayed because He knew His Father was with Him and loved Him. He prayed because He loved His Father more than Himself. He prayed because He desperately wanted to hear from Him. It was like breathing air to Him.

Is Jesus our example and blueprint? I believe that He is. He is the perfect picture of what we were made for and recreated to be. We were also made for our Heavenly Father and talking with Him *is* the most natural thing that we could find ourselves doing.

Thinking about prayer as a discipline leads to making prayer about <u>us</u> and not about our <u>love relationship</u> with our Creator. *If we continue with this thinking, we will see prayer as a <u>task</u> and inevitably lead us to burnout.* Our prayers will be limited to how disciplined we are.

When prayer is about our relationship with God who pursues us and loves us, then we can constantly be in communication with Him regardless of how disciplined we are. This will never lead to burnout. For how could we burn out on hearing from and talking to God when that is exactly what we're designed to do?

OUT WITH THE OLD, IN WITH THE NEW

Can you join me in getting rid of the term "spiritual discipline" from our Christian vocabulary and replace it? Let's swap it out for a more appropriate term—*"spiritual pleasures."* I think this is a better description because these activities are *supposed to be* enjoyable *and pleasurable.*

Isn't that why God prescribed these things in the first place? They are for our enjoyment and not a weight to carry or a chore to accomplish. Like the first commands given to Adam and Eve, God instructs us to do these things because they are natural and for our enjoyment.

MORE FREEDOM

When we make these changes in our vocabulary and thinking, they will transform how we approach and experience all the spiritual pleasures. Do you see that you don't need to climb the mountains of prayer, Bible reading, fasting, etc.?

The Christian life is not about striving, training and disciplining ourselves. Instead, the Christian life is filled with good things that God instructs us to do and are freeing and natural. They aren't meant to be burdensome tasks to check off our "to-do list"!

Having lived on the other side for so long, I can understand if it's difficult to take it all in. Once we remove the performance veil that's been covering our eyes, it's hard to adjust to the light.

A BRAND NEW DAY!

Viewing commands like "love one another" as natural and easy is a departure from how we've been accustomed to understanding doing good works. Even though it's challenging to change our perspective on following the things the Bible instructs us to do, we *must* make the adjustment.

If we don't replace our old way of thinking with a correct view of living, then we'll have no other recourse than to return to PBT. As we've noted, life is full of things to do, so we must have a Biblical lens to assess our performance.

To help make this change, let's look at one more example. The principle that I developed was a breakthrough moment concerning reading the Bible and went a long way in transforming my thinking.

THE HUNGER PRINCIPLE

Start by thinking about a time when you didn't open up the Bible for an extended period. Maybe it was a week, two weeks or months. However long it was for you, picture yourself back at this time.

Now during this season, try to recall what you were feeling every time you looked at the Bible sitting on your table or bookshelf. If you are like me, each time you looked at the Bible, you had an awful feeling stir inside.

How did I interpret that feeling in the past? I interpreted it as guilt. I felt extremely guilty for not being in God's word. I knew I should pick up the Bible and read it, but I left it sitting there.

No matter how hard it was to pick up the Bible, eventually I would push myself to do it. I would break through my inertia because my disdain of the heavy, guilt-laden feeling I had.

When I would finally get myself to crack open my Bible, often I wouldn't get much out of it. But that didn't matter. I was still glad that I read the Bible, because at least I got rid of the guilty feeling.

It was during one of these times when God started to speak to me. He asked me if this was how I was supposed to approach reading His word. Was it ok that I was reading the Bible to rid myself of this guilty feeling? Was this supposed to be my motivation to read the Bible? The answer was clearly NO!

What God revealed to me next radically changed my whole view. He showed me that the discomfort I felt after not reading the Bible was not guilt, it was actually hunger. *What I was interpreting as guilt was actually my hunger to be with Him.*

As we discussed with prayer, God designed us to be in communion with Him. When we are not spending time with Him, it's only *natural* that we are going to miss being with Him. We are going to feel hungry for God's presence again.

This is similar to when we are away from those that we love for an extended period of time. It could be a conference, business trip or our kids being at a camp, but being away from our loved ones leaves us with a longing and hunger to be reconnected with them.

When we're apart from them, we have this unsettled feeling inside. Yet when we have that feeling stir within our hearts, we don't interpret it as guilt. We correctly interpret that as a longing or hunger to be reunited with those we love.

Shouldn't that also be true with the One that we were destined and created to be with forever? When we are apart from Him, we should be feeling hunger to reconnect. *This hunger should be the primary driving force for us to read God's word and spend time with Him.* This is the hunger principle and it represented a big change in how I viewed reading the Bible.

THE BREAD OF LIFE

To further develop this idea of the hunger principle, God brought to mind the words of Jesus in Matthew 4:4:

> Jesus answered, "It is written: 'Man shall not live on bread alone, but on every word that comes from the mouth of God.'"

Jesus is comparing God's word to bread. He is making the assertion that God's word and hearing from Him are our sustenance. In relating God's word to physical food, Jesus is using an analogy that's relatable.

Just as our bodies hunger for physical food, our spiritual bodies also hunger for the "bread of life" when we don't spend time eating at God's table.

THE REFRIGERATOR DOOR

Let's say there was a day when you were extremely busy and you had to rush off without eating breakfast. You were so busy at work or school, you just didn't have time to eat lunch or dinner. You get home in the evening and you realize that you haven't eaten all day long. Then you feel some rumbling in your gut.

What is that rumbling? Of course, you know what this is. It's guilt! You feel remorse that you haven't eaten all day. It's your *responsibility* to feed your body, so you are racked with guilt.

You think about going to the refrigerator, but you can't do it. You know you *should* open the refrigerator door, but it's *too hard*. You can't muster the energy to open the fridge and get something to eat, so you tell yourself that maybe you'll get to it tomorrow.

Ridiculous? Nonsensical? Of course, it is. We know instinctively that the feeling we have inside is hunger. When we don't eat, our stomach rumbles and cries out, "I need food!" We don't misinterpret this feeling inside as guilt.

Yet isn't this exactly how we approach reading the Bible? When we don't spend time with God and feel some rumbling inside, we interpret it as guilt. We need to see that what we are actually experiencing is hunger pains. It's our longing to be with the One we were created for.

SET FREE

This new way of thinking set me free. Now, whenever I sense that unsettled feeling from not reading the Bible, I correctly identify it as hunger. And what do you do when you are hungry? You eat.

When we feel hungry physically, we instinctively open the fridge and get something to eat. It's easy and natural. Not only that, but when we are really hungry, the food we eat tastes especially good! It becomes the best meal that we've ever had.

That's exactly how we are supposed to react when we feel spiritually hungry. We just eat. No heavy burden. No being overcome with guilt, obligation or shame. No more summoning up enough energy to try and open up the Bible. When you are really hungry because you've spent a long time away from His word, you will enjoy it that much more.

That's the freedom that God brought with the hunger principle. I no longer have to discipline myself to spend time with Him. I wake up in the morning hungry to be with Him, so I eat. I just respond to my hunger.

I don't read because I have to. I read because I WANT to. I want to not because it's become a habit, but because I desperately want to be with Jesus. It's no longer a task or about performance. It's about being with the One I love and the One who loves me.

LATE-NIGHT SNACK

I shared this hunger principle one day with a person that I had been mentoring. When I saw him the following week, he had this excited look on his face and told me that he had a cool story that he wanted to share with me. It piqued my interest.

He started sharing about something that happened earlier that week. He shared how it was late at night and he felt hungry. Then he got up and went to have a snack. He paused and smiled at me. I was thinking my friend had lost it. Why was he smiling at me about having a snack in the middle of the night?

He probably noticed the bewildered look on my face, so he reminded me that we had talked about the hunger principle the week before. That night he told me that he recognized that he was hungry, so he went to go eat. It wasn't him having an "official quiet time." He was just hungry, so he went to read and pray. I started to smile. He got it!

DON'T GET RID OF THAT!

Do you feel the room spinning? Has all this change in thinking messed with your equilibrium? Well hold on, we're not done yet! When God started showing me about the hunger principle, He took it up a notch.

As God began showing me that this unsettled feeling inside when I was apart from Him was actually hunger pains, I had this sobering thought. *I had spent my entire Christian life driven to rid myself of this feeling that God intended for my good.* Because I misinterpreted this hunger as guilt, I had tried my best to run away from it. I did everything I could to make it go away. What was God thinking while watching me do this time and again?

Because of my PBT I had made reading the Bible a task. When I didn't do it, it produced what I thought was guilt. *But all along this hunger was something that God put within me. It was His homing beacon, the longing He wove into each of us to be with Him and Him alone.* And I was trying to turn it off!

Now that I recognize that, I don't try to escape. Instead I try to step into it. I try to embrace the stirring within me and see that it's my built-in hunger to be with the lover of my soul. Yet again, God was redeeming what I thought was a negative into a positive.

Because I can correctly interpret the internal stirrings, I find myself reading the Bible more consistently than I ever have. I can do this because I'm not weighed down by guilt and I'm spurred on by my hunger.

But more than that I am enjoying reading the Bible more than I ever have. It's no longer a discipline. It's a time to be with the One that I want to be with and hear from.

I do realize that this is a giant change in our paradigm. I recognize that I'm asking you to throw out everything that you might have thought to be true about spiritual discipline. But if you can adjust your thinking and embrace the truth, it will turn discipline into delight.

When the false guilt and heavy weight are taken away, you will be left to enjoy. You will make following the commands a joy knowing that you are just being who God created and designed you to be.

Let's sum up by looking at how we should view things like praying and reading the Bible.

Spending time with God is our:

- **Design not discipline**
- **Hunger not habit**
- **Desire not duty**

We need to swap out our flesh-driven engines with spirit-designed engines to drive us to do exactly what we're created for. Let's keep up the momentum towards greater freedom in Christ!

Note: Before we move onto the last section of the bonus material, I want to point out one more time that doing this is not easy. It's not easy to change the thinking that we might have been carrying for our entire lives.

Even if we change our thinking, it's <u>still</u> not going to always be easy. It's difficult to maintain things like reading the Bible and praying, not because these activities are difficult, but because of circumstances, our brokenness, our past PBT, or other issues beyond our control. What is in our control? It's what we choose to listen to and believe.

I wanted to stop and acknowledge these things because adjusting our thinking will take time. It took months for me to adjust to this new way of thinking. It wasn't always easy *nor* did it feel natural. But eventually it does work! Not just because I have experienced it, but because it's God's design for these things to be natural and enjoyable for us.

GOD'S NOT DUMB!

Remember when we talked about God forgiving all our sin upfront? We pointed out that it's difficult for us to understand how God forgives because we don't forgive everyone's sin upfront. But we need to ask the question, "*Why don't we do that? Why don't we forgive everyone's sin upfront?*"

Maybe we feel like it'll give people the license to run all over us and take advantage of the free pass we are giving them. Then doesn't God worry about this? Isn't He concerned that by forgiving all our sins upfront that we'll take advantage of His grace?

Isn't He worried that we'll run rampant and be sinning nonstop knowing full well that He's already forgiven all our sins? What's to stop us from sinning all the time when God already makes it clear that Jesus paid for all our sins past, present and future?

Well, He doesn't worry because He is always in control and He's not dumb! God knows what He's doing. He doesn't worry because He has made some provisions. First, He has made us new creations. Our old self was bent away from God (dead to Him), the Christian's new self is aligned towards God (alive to Him).

That is very important. If God gave us this forgiveness and had *not* made us new creations that are drawn towards him, then we'd have the potential to run wild. *We need to see that God has more faith in who we are and what He's done than we do.*

He knows that He's made a fundamental change in who we are. He knows that at the core of our new identity the Christian is not made for sin any longer (see Romans 6:11). We are made for Him. We are restored to our original design, which is made by Him and for Him.

GUILTY EVIDENCE

In fact, when we do feel guilt after sin, it can actually be a sign that God has transformed us. After we've sinned, we can sense there's a problem. Internally, we feel that this is not good. Typically, we interpret this unsettled feeling as guilt. *But maybe* we should see this as evidence that God has made a funda-mental change within us.

You see, we are no longer geared towards sin, so when we do sin, we _should feel that something is not right_. But maybe what we've thought of as guilt is ac-tually conviction. Whereas guilt is unbiblical for the Christian, conviction is very appropriate. Maybe we need to make a change in how we see and label what's happening internally when we sin.

Similar to the hunger principle, it's our old pattern of thinking that assigns a "guilty" tag to what we are feeling. But for the Christian, we need to rename this feeling we have after committing a sin. We need to see that it's actually conviction that we are feeling. This conviction is evidence of something good.

This is evidence that we have the Holy Spirit living within us. It is evidence that God has made a change to our identity. We need to reinterpret our feelings, from guilt to conviction.

You see, God is not dumb. He has not set things in motion that will inevitably fail. He has not given his children a free pass to run wild. He *has* made changes to our very nature.

He has given us the Holy Spirit. He has given us conviction. He has given us this internal sensor to point out that sin is not what we are built and designed for. He's also given us one more thing.

THAT WILL WORK!

Inherent with God's forgiveness and having dealt with our sin is the fact that we now are able to enter into His presence with confidence (see Hebrews 4:14-16). God dealt with sin, guilt and shame so that we can be with Him. He provided forgiveness of sin to enable us to walk into the throne room and be with the King, our Heavenly Father.

Why is this helpful? Because *sin is a substitute*. When we have the real thing and are filled by God, then we no longer have the need for a substitute. When our spirit and soul feel complete and fulfilled, sin loses its allure. What tempted us before no longer has as much pull.

That's why the old way of dealing with sin and repentance is so ineffective. Take a look at the diagram from the previous chapter on repentance again, but we will add one more thing:

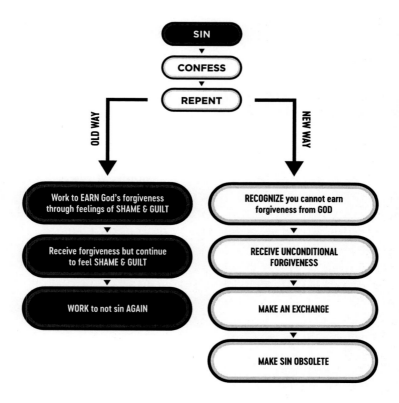

First, let's look at the left side, the old way of dealing with sin through guilt and earning forgiveness. This old way doesn't allow us to feel God's love and presence in the midst of our sin and failure (because of PBT).

When we experience forgiveness based on our actions, it will be difficult to have a sense that God loves us *unconditionally*. We can't. We can't because we will never feel right about God's presence with us after we've failed Him.

We can't sense God's presence because He shouldn't bless us in this way after we've sinned. Confessing sin and failure leading to God's forgiveness, love and presence? That just doesn't compute.

That's why we are left to our own devices to combat sin. If we don't receive God's forgiveness and resulting presence, what do we have left to help us combat sin? We have ourselves. We have our own determination to not sin again. We have our guilt and shame. We want to avoid guilt and shame, so we try to avoid sin.

It doesn't take long to realize that self-reliance doesn't work. We will never have lasting victory over sin unless we have and experience His presence and love, which is the antidote to sin.

The key is to make sin obsolete (see last step of the New Way). If we have what we were designed for (God), then what use is a substitute (sin)? Instead of making our focus not sinning, our focus should be giving our soul what it is truly hungering for.

The only way to experience more of God's unconditional love and presence is to free yourself from the old way of dealing with repentance (based on PBT). Then exchange this old way with a new way. This new way is centered on upfront forgiveness and unconditional love instead of guilt and shame.

God knows that we will still sin. But He has given us a new identity, His presence and love, to combat sin in our lives. He's offered forgiveness all upfront because He's not dumb. He's changed us and empowered us to live the life He intended. The question is then: "Do we believe it?"

Are we willing to let go of the old way? Are we willing to accept God's forgiveness without trying to earn it with our feelings of guilt and shame? Are we willing to accept what Jesus did and not add to or redo what He's already done?

Can you accept forgiveness even though you don't deserve it? Can you receive it even though you can't pay him back? Can you allow yourself to take it in without trying to earn it? Can you allow yourself to be accepted and loved unconditionally?

These are not rhetorical questions. What I'm asking is not that simple. When I tried to pursue this new route, I fought it tooth and nail. Every fiber of my being shouted that this was not right.

Sin, repent and then just receive? No more guilt? No more shame? No more promises? No more rationalizing my sin? No more beating myself up? No more earning? No more making myself feel better about receiving? Can this be right? Yes, it is! These is the amazing truth and power of the gospel message.

THAT'S WHAT YOU WERE THINKING?

Let's close this section by hearing from God. Let's hear what God says about our sin and repentance. The following is what I imagine God thinking about our past experience with sin and repentance:

"Why are you coming to me wondering if you are going to be forgiven? Why are you asking me to forgive something that I've already forgiven? Do you think that I'm surprised that you committed this particular sin?

Do you think that I didn't realize you'd commit this sin when I forgave all your sins upfront? Do think this one caught me off guard? Those other sins I forgave, but not this one?

NO, you don't have to do that. You don't have to show me how horrible your sin was because Jesus already did. Jesus showed me how tragic your sin was.

My son's death demonstrated how serious your sin was to me. You actually have no idea how serious your sin was. But Jesus did, and He still bears the scars to prove it.

Jesus took all the guilt and shame with Him to the cross. You don't need to carry that anymore. Jesus already did. Can you receive what He's done for you? Are you going to let your performance-based thinking (yes, God knows about PBT) prevent you from receiving my grace and mercy?

I love you and have taken you in despite your sin. Are you going to continue looking in from the outside? Or are you going to drop your performance-based, earning-based thinking long enough to come in and receive the wonderful gift Jesus and I have given you? Are you going to come into my throne room and be in my presence even after you sin?

After you sin again, will you receive the work of the cross and come be with me? I want to be with you. That's why I had to send my one and only Son. Jesus didn't want to endure the pain of being separated from me when I laid the sin of the world on Him. He prayed for that cup to pass.

But it was my love for you, my consuming desire to be with you that caused me to follow through with being separated from my Son. Drop your PBT. Come in. Be loved and unconditionally accepted by your Heavenly Father."

This is the message God wants to convey to us. We need to drop the false idea that He bases forgiveness on our worthiness and performance. You cannot and could not ever do anything to deserve God's forgiveness. We need to stop trying.

We should recognize that we are undeserving, but at the same time we simply need to receive. We don't need to show God how serious we think our sin is, He already knows. He knows the cost.

Even if we don't spend time beating ourselves up, it doesn't mean we are taking sin lightly. We can realize what Jesus had to pay in order to deal with our sin. We can recognize the gravity of His sacrifice.

Instead of pouring energy into dealing with guilt and shame, we should focus our efforts on receiving the fruit of what Jesus has done for us. We should receive the heart of our Father. We need to be loved. We need to let God love us unconditionally *during* repentance.

If you've spent a lifetime not receiving but being condemned through repentance, this will be an adjustment for you. It will feel unnatural to do. This was my experience. But this where we must let the truth drive our actions and not our past experience or feelings. Follow the truth, and our feelings will follow.

WHAT ABOUT MY LIFE?

1. Describe your experience or struggle trying to maintain a consistent prayer life or reading the Bible. What would change if you stopped making these activities tasks?

2. Have you felt God's homing beacon go off inside? You might have interpreted it as guilt. What would happen if you didn't try to get rid of it but actually embraced this discontent and hunger you felt inside when you didn't spend time with God?

3. Have you tried to battle sin through your own determination and trying to avoid guilt and shame? Describe if that has been successful or not. How would things change if you switched your strategy to making sin obsolete (through being loved and believing your new identity)?

Let me close with this. It's the truth that we are loved. You may have grown accustomed to hearing this if you've grown up going to church, but if you have never *truly* experienced it, let this hit you anew.

We need to know this *not just in our heads but in our hearts. Feelings are not supposed to lead. But feelings should follow the truth*. If it's true that you are really loved, we should actually *feel* loved. This is vital to our becoming free.

You will never be able to fully let God take control if you don't trust Him. If you are not secure, you'll never feel safe enough to let God completely take control. But this is exactly what we need to do. Remember this is the ultimate freedom we can have in this life.

When we are loved, we will be free. When we give God space to act on our behalf, we will feel more secure. It's from a place of security that we can let go of more control. Our greatest joy will come when God can be God in our lives instead of us trying to take His place.

When we become Christians, this is what we prayed to do. We prayed that Jesus would be our Savior and **Lord over our lives**. When we let go of our PBT, we can see this prayer be answered. It is not through our effort but by trusting God's.

God loves you. By giving up your performance-based thinking, He will demonstrate His love, power, peace, joy and fruitfulness. You can and will have the most fulfilling and free life that Jesus died to give you!

Now, go *BE FREE*!

NOTES

NOTES